FROM FLIPPING BURGERS TO FLIPPING BILLIONS

JAMES HATTON JR.

Print ISBN: 978-1-944066-43-7

The information provided in this book is for informational purposes only and is not intended to be a source of advice or credit analysis with respect to the material presented. The information and/or documents contained in this book do not constitute legal, financial, or health advice and should never be used without first consulting with a licensed professional to determine what may be best for your individual needs.

The publisher and the author do not make any guarantee or other promise as to any results that may be obtained from using the content of this book. You should never make any decision without first consulting with your own professional and licensed advisor and conducting your own research and due diligence. To the maximum extent permitted by law, the publisher and the author disclaim any and all liability in the event any information, commentary, analysis, opinions, advice, and/or recommendations contained in this book prove to be inaccurate, incomplete or unreliable or result in any investment or other losses.

Content contained or made available through this book is not intended to and does not constitute licensed advice, and no client relationship is formed. The publisher and the author are providing this book and its contents on an "as is" basis. Your use of the information in this book is at your own risk.

I have tried to recreate events, locales, and conversations from my memories of them. In order to maintain their anonymity in some instances, I have changed the names of individuals and places. I may have changed some identifying characteristics and details such as physical properties, occupations and places of residence.

Although the author and publisher have made every effort to ensure that the information in this book was correct at press time, the author and publisher do not assume and hereby disclaim any liability to any party for any loss, damage, or disruption caused by errors or omissions, whether such errors or omissions result from negligence, accident, or any other cause.

Contents

Introduction

In preparing for this book, I was reminded how important single days can be. Our lives can change, good or bad, between a sunrise and sunset. Gathering materials for a book like this is simply collecting the stories from those days and putting them down on a page—that is the easy part. The hard part of the process is understanding why those days are important to you and to me. I wish I could only tell you about the fun days of birthday parties and successful business ventures. If I did that, you would miss out on the most important stories of my life. Those are the stories of where I stumbled. Imagine me at the little kid that has been told not to touch the hot oven but does it anyway. The child does not understand what touching the stove will do to his finger until he does it. The good news is that once burned, the child is less likely to touch a hot surface again. In writing about the parts of my life that are not so pretty, I hope I can be that stove-touching child for you. As you read about my struggles, you might avoid some of those snares that snagged me up.

One of the biggest burdens in my life is a gambling addiction. My first bet was for good intentions. I saw an easy way to get myself out of a business-related financial jam on a sure thing. The money I laid down on that first bet multiplied like rabbits, and I came away a winner. What did that bet hurt? I had made the bet on an overseas internet site where sports betting was legal. It was not like I went to some back alley and made a bet with a bookie who preyed on the members of my community. I had made what I needed to make and that was it. I would not need to turn to gambling to cover my business' shortfalls. Next time, I would know better. I told myself it was a one-time thing—it was not.

I thought that meeting the need for fast money was the only factor at work in my mind—it was not. There is a winner's rush that comes from a group of chemicals released in your brain called endorphins. These chemicals both make you feel good and block pain. As a matter of fact, endorphins are a minor opioid and react with the body just like oxycontin does. Your body releases endorphins for many different reasons. You might have heard of a runner's high. That is when exercise triggers the body to produce endorphins. I wish I had gone for a run to catch my next endorphin buzz. I rationalized the next bet and the next, until gambling was as much a part of my life as breathing.

I started this work before the COVID-19 crisis of 2020, and one of those important days happened during the autumn of that year. On November 1, 2020, sports betting became legal in my home state of Tennessee. Over the next few months, I started to see the effect legalized gambling had on my community. I would talk to young brothers who would be excited about their winnings on a Sunday night. I would talk to some of those winners the next week and they would wonder where they were going to get that month's rent payment. The events of November 1, 2020, solidified the need for me to finish this work. I needed to testify to the world how gambling had affected my life.

The cautionary tale of my gambling addiction is only half the story. The other half is the hope my story can bring. No matter how much or little you have in this world, determination and hard work do pay off. I was literally flipping burgers at two different fast-food restaurants to pay for real estate investments. I lived as lean as I could so I could make my dream of becoming a real estate developer come true. I want everyone to understand that if I can do it, so can you. You might have to make some sacrifices and change your habits, but you can make a better life for yourself.

The final lesson I wish for you to take away from this text is that no matter how badly you think you have made a mess of your life—you can turn things around. There is no situation that you cannot overcome with the right mindset, help from others, and faith in God. We have no greater example than Saint Paul on the road to Damascus to illuminate our path. The process for Paul reinventing himself and aligning to a righteous way included being blind for a time. During those dark days of our lives, when all seems lost, we will be in the dark too. When we take one step at a time towards our own path to righteousness, we are working toward a better tomorrow. We might not always walk that path at the pace we wish, but with faith, we will get to where the Lord wants us to be.

I have seen how making better decisions, leaning on my Brothers and Sisters, and trusting in a higher calling works in my life. From my waking nightmare days drenched with bet after bet, I had to start over. I went back to where I started from and reminded myself of the fundamentals you will read about in this book. Even as these words are being written, I have multiple investments in both real estate and the stock market. I keep my eye on the disciplined decisions that I know create success in my life. For example, my dream car is a 2021 Mercedes Benz Maybach. I could get a car loan tomorrow and drive one off the lot, but I have not. I still drive my dependable 2000 Honda hoopty. The money I save on a car payment, I put towards more investments that will secure a better future for myself and my family.

We live in perilous times. Aside from the dangers to one's personal health the COVID-19 crisis has inflicted on us, the rush to minimize the economic impact can be hurtful too. There are those who are looking to take advantage of no foreclosure edicts, stimulus checks, and COVID impact business loans. These programs are intended to help those in need but could start some bad financial habits. Just because your landlord cannot foreclose on you does not mean you can stop paying your rent. The bill will come due one day. It is better, if you are able, to use those momentary advantages to get ahead of the game or invest. Sometimes it takes a little wisdom on the front end to make more money on the back end. Use that stimulus money to pay off a credit card or other debt. Look to the future and not the present.

I want my future, and yours, to be easier than it has in years past. I want all of us to wake up every morning with a sense of purpose of marching toward our dreams. Along the way, I want everyone to lend a hand to those in our lives that need a leg up or a broad shoulder to lean on. I want you to forgive yourself for your missteps and learn from your mistakes instead of beating yourself up over them. I pray you take my examples, both good and bad, and let them assist you.

God bless you on your path,
James Hatton

Chapter One
Growing Up

I grew up and still live in Columbia, Tennessee. Situated halfway between Nashville and Huntsville, Alabama, Columbia is exactly what you would expect out of a Southern town. The beauty of the surrounding countryside cannot make up for the sins of the past and present. Through most of the town's modern history, the town's main industry was tobacco and hemp. The city's economy began to change during World War II as phosphate mining and the supporting chemical industry settled in to support the war effort. The infrastructure that was built in and around

Columbia for the chemical industry would pay off in the next four decades. Interstate 65 (I-65) was routed through Columbia connecting the city to a highway reaching from the Great Lakes to the Gulf of Mexico. Up until the 1980s, Columbia's claim to fame was the annual Mule Day festival. Starting in the 1840s, Mule Day was a gathering for mule breeders to swap stories and bloodlines. The festival has turned into a full-fledged country jamboree with home cooking, flea markets, dancing, music, and of course, mule competitions.

The quaint country charm of Columbia quickly began to change in 1986 when General Motors (GM) announced they would be breaking ground on an automotive factory just up in the road in Spring Hill, Tennessee. To compete with Japanese automakers, GM's new facility would produce the Saturn line of cars. Everything about the car-making process was reimagined with Saturn. From a just-in-time inventory model for parts to encouraging smaller vendors to relocate nearby, Saturn was destined to change the way America made cars. When the first Saturn rolled off the assembly line in 1990, Spring Hill and Columbia had already been changed forever.

There probably was not a single person in Maury County that the prosperity of Saturn did not touch. From breaking ground to producing cars in four short years means a lot of stress on a small country town and the area's new transplants. GM moved a hefty number of their Detroit employees down South to support the build and subsequent factory operations. The transplants from Motor City did not just bring new ideas with them. They also brought their vices. Everything from prostitution to drugs landed on Columbia nearly overnight. The same roadways and interstate that made Maury County attractive to GM were also mainline for human and drug trafficking. Where there are drugs and prostitution, violence is not far behind. Murder and drive-by shootings became as common in Columbia as last year's Mule Day posters. The city's police department, even today, struggles to keep up with a crime rate that is higher than 83 percent of other cities in the United States.[1]

General Motors never quite lived up to its promises of reinvigorating the automotive industry. While the Saturn plant was a model for efficiency, customers did not take to the car line as GM had hoped. Since the mid-2000s, the Spring Hill facility has gone through several ups and downs that continue to yo-yo the local economy. The fading light of Saturn is when I grew up in Columbia. The small-time Detroit gangsters that invaded the city twenty years before had taught a new generation life on the street. It was, and is, as easy to get in the game on the streets of Columbia, Tennessee as it is in New York or Los Angeles. I had friends and family members caught up in that mess. It never ends well, and I could have been caught up in it too.

The example of my family undoubtedly kept me out of trouble growing up. My mother and father are two of the hardest working people I have ever known. They both grew up in Maury County and saw the same number and type of difficulties that have landed on their neighbors. I think the difference is my parents decided not to leave their fate in the hands of someone else. My parents believe in hard work and self-reliance. With whatever setbacks my folks had, they never asked anyone for anything. They have never accepted any form of public assistance. I doubt even if the circumstances were dire, they would take a handout from anyone. They have never had the need to do so. For as long as I can remember, both of my parents have worked two jobs. That was their form of financial diversification. If one job went away, they could live on the other. Having the freedom of choice also allows you to stand up for yourself.

My mother always worked two jobs in the fast-food industry and stood up for herself no matter what the cost. She is as polite a person as they come, but one day a customer came in who was not satisfied with her service. The customer was of the "good ol' boy" variety and started in on my mother, eventually calling her a nigger. The sins of the past have not died in Maury County, as I mentioned before. Racism is alive in Columbia. Within my grandparents' lifetime, there have been lynchings and other race-related violence in my own and my parent's lifetimes. Mom still gave as good as she got to the customer. You would think that standing up for yourself and putting a racist in their place would have been rewarded by the restaurant's management. Instead, mom was told she handled the situation poorly and was fired for her trouble. The city of Columbia's motto, "Old South charm, new South progress—something good around every corner" does not always ring true.

If my mother taught me a moral backbone, my father taught me to have a physically strong back. He worked in a factory as his primary job and then had a side hustle as a stonemason. Imagine getting off one physically demanding job to create works of architectural art with heavy slabs of rock. I think my father is incapable of stopping work or quitting at anything. That is another example I have always wished to live up to.

If I learned to stick up for myself and a work ethic from my parents, my frugal entrepreneurial spirit came from my grandfather. He was something of a character. He owned some rental properties throughout Columbia, but he always had something else going. He worked and lived at one of the town's funeral homes. Someone had to be there overnight if a body came in. The funeral home was a free place for him to live, and he got paid too. So even though he owned several properties, my grandfather continued to live above the funeral home to save money. If managing properties and working at a funeral home was not enough, my grandfather had a side hustle. Most days you could see him at the courthouse selling pocketknives. I wish I had one of those knives today.

My grandfather had more going on than just work. He had twenty-two children and took care of every one of them. Aside from the normal costs of upbringing, my grandfather had a larger goal.

He was a real estate man too and wanted to give each of his children a home if he could. At the least, my grandfather wanted to supply the down payment for a house. Having aspirations like that goes beyond parental care. My grandfather had a sense of legacy he wanted to fulfill. I do not believe that legacy was out of a selfish need for remembrance. I think my grandfather understood the secret behind real estate is that homes and property are where memories are made. Just like recognizing the importance of days, remembering where things happened is of importance too. There is no doubt that my grandfather wanted to give his children a safe and secure place to create memories with their families.

My grandmother had her own version of legacy-making that was more personal than my grandfather's. She, above anyone else, was the biggest influence on me growing up. Since my parents were always working, my grandmother raised me. She got me ready and fed me breakfast every morning. After the dishes were cleared from the table, she would walk me a few blocks to school. She would be standing on the sidewalk waiting for me when school let out. Rain or shine, my grandmother was always there. When I was young, I did not understand the full reason she walked me to and from school.

I did not have the eyes to see what was going on outside that safe path my grandmother walked me on every day. My neighborhood had seen the worst of the big-city vices that hit Columbia. There was everything from crack houses to gangs and shootings happening in a few-block radius of my house and school. Columbia's drug problem hit closer to home than my route home from school. I had an uncle who was convicted on drug-related charges. I don't know if I ever was told the full story with that, but my grandmother kept me away from all of that. I am sure that I never got approached by older kids who would have led me into trouble, because my grandmother was there with me every step of the way.

My grandmother's legacy was to keep me safe and to give me the space to grow without bad influences. Outside of that, there were also the pearls of wisdom my grandmother left with me. Possibly the most important piece of advice she gave me was, "You can't trust anyone with money." I would regret not listening to a few years later in one of my real estate deals. Most of the other adages she gave me were on how to handle matters of the heart. I was a little too young to fathom the havoc young ladies can wreak on a boy's life. All I knew was that I should smile, nod, and be polite to the grandmother who was desperately trying to keep the world from tainting her grandson.

High School

Trouble can find all of us sooner or later. Mine would not find me until a few years down the line. Until then, I was playing basketball and trying to graduate high school. I, like most of my classmates, was not that interested in the coursework. Given the rough streets most of my classmates were coming from, it is no wonder that education was not a top priority. The indifference from the student body hit the teachers too. I remember one day my social studies teacher, Mr. Bobo, got fed up with everyone. Bobo had had enough of everyone playing around.

He calmly told the class, "All of y'all that don't want to be here can go roam the halls. I do not care what you do. School is not for everyone. Get out of here and go work for yourself."

When Mr. Bobo had his say, I was not quite old enough to have a job. His words always stuck with me on a broader scale. First, if I am not happy with where I am at and what I am doing, I should be doing something different. Secondly, would it not be better to work for me and make my own rules rather than having to abide by someone else's? It sure sounded like roaming the halls looking for my own way was much better than the alternatives.

Another high school teacher of mine reinforced how I interpreted Mr. Bobo's words, but not in the way you would think. Mrs. Porter, a math teacher, was unimpressed with my scholarly efforts. I cannot remember what I was doing, but Mrs. Porter stopped in the middle of class to dress me down in front of everyone.

"James, if you don't start paying attention, you're not going to amount to anything."

To this day, I am not sure if Mrs. Porter was trying to embarrass me or light a fire under my backside. As much as Mrs. Porter's words stung, I knew they could not be true. I already had plans and dreams. Mrs. Porter's words made me want to succeed even more than ever. The best revenge would be years later to drive up to my high school reunion in a brand-new car. I would tell everyone about my accomplishments as a real estate developer and how I had used my grandfather's methods to start my empire. Whatever her reasoning, I owe Mrs.

Porter a bit of thanks for keeping me going during some dark times.

Since it was not years later, at a reunion, I started to tell my friends about my dreams. My buddy Tina Jones heard me talk about real estate so often, she got sick of it. I believe there was one point she forbade me from talking about real estate anymore. The funny thing is Tina would become a successful real estate developer years later. The things you say do matter to the people around you. Even though we have stayed in touch over the years, I do not know if my jabbering about real estate influenced her career choice or not. What I do know is that those around you listen and take your words to heart even when you do not think they are listening. I also know that Tina is a true friend who believed in me when I did not think anyone else would. She loaned me the seed money for a real estate deal I would make years later.

You can never underestimate the impact you will have on someone else's life, or you will have on theirs. My best friend in high school was James Jacks III. We got plenty of ribbing for being James and James, but we were pretty much inseparable in those days. James did make an impression on me as an individual of character. If this tells you anything about him, James is currently based in Germany with the U.S. Air Force. He is set to retire with twenty years of service to our country soon and come home to new challenges. But back then, we were just kids looking forward to everything in the world that did not have to do with school.

By the time we were fifteen, I was always over at James's house to hang out, spend the night, or to have dinner. James's parents told me that if I wanted to that summer, I could go with them to visit their extended family in Detroit. If I wanted? I was not what you would call well-traveled, so a road trip to Detroit sounded like a huge adventure. There was the matter of spending money and getting clothes for the trip. The state of Tennessee allowed a fifteen-year-old to hold down a part-time job. The restrictions imposed by the state limited the number of hours and times I could work. That was fine with me as long as I could make money.

My First Job

Truth be told, I carried two different first jobs. Even then, I took the example of my parents and grandfather to heart. Whenever I could, I was sacking groceries at a local supermarket. It was not especially difficult work, and I sometimes got tips taking groceries out to someone's car. I wasn't too enthusiastic when I went into that job. James's mom caught on and suggest an alternative. James's mother worked in the human resources department at Nashville's Vanderbilt Medical Center. She suggested that James and I apply at the McDonald's in the hospital. She took us for our interviews and the two Jameses were hired on for the summer.

In those days, McDonald's was in a brick courtyard of the hospital. The open space had benches for people to sit among planters filled with greenery. It felt like this open space was the center point of the hospital. Doctors and nurses in scrubs and lab coats would scurry from the buildings the courtyard connected. There were always the smokers hanging around too. The medical staff tried to slink in corners to hide their bad habits from their peers. Then there were the smokers who were obviously visiting someone in the hospital. They had a thousand-yard stare and looked like they had no joy in either being outside or smoking. Their minds were elsewhere on loved ones whose lives might have hung in the balance. One commonality it seemed that everyone had was McDonald's was a touchstone for everyone. There is comfort in the familiar and exhausted emotionally charged people cling to stability. "You deserve a break today" was still a McDonald's ad campaign, and I could tell that most everyone who entered the restaurant could use a pause.

It felt like everyone who entered the boundaries of Vanderbilt Medical Center ended up coming to McDonald's. That was on a normal day, but Wednesdays were the worst. On Wednesdays McDonald's ran a twenty-nine-cent hamburger and thirty-nine-cent cheeseburger promotion. We started serving the lunch menu at 10:30 AM and by 10:31, we had orders stacking up. When I was there that first summer, I do not think the kitchen's air conditioner worked on a single Wednesday. Nashville's normally hot and humid summer days mixed with blazing grills and fryers make the kitchen nearly unbearable. The combination of grease, grilled onions, and the close-quartered crew's body odor stuck to you like someone had wrapped you in plastic wrap. It was impossible for your eyebrows to keep the sweat out of your eyes. At times you could barely see what you were doing because of it.

Even with the hardships fast food brought, I did like the work. There was always something that needed doing, and I was a fast learner. I took every opportunity I could to find out how to do something different. Breaking down the shake machine (that only worked half the time to begin with), making a new sandwich, or inventorying stock did not matter to me. What mattered was I could see the good I was doing at the restaurant. My crew members depended on me and I came through for them.

I also knew that working for McDonald's made more sense than Mrs. Porter's math class. Contributing while I was making money, that was the only equation I needed. I kept working and putting money aside even while I was in high school. I knew that one day I would need the funds to fuel my dreams. That day would come sooner than I expected.

Chapter Two
Early Days

If you were playing the party game Three Facts and a Lie with me, you might think that "not finishing high school" was the lie. I wish it wasn't, but I never graduated. The reasons for not getting my high school diploma aren't as important as what I did after. I've always believed that not all forms of education need classrooms and homework. There's also not a connection between intelligence and formal education or station in life. Some of the drug dealers I grew up with were smarter than CEOs and real estate developers I have met. What matters in someone's life aren't the diplomas or certificates that hang on your wall. What matters is what you do with your life.

So there I was, fully in charge of my life after high school. I had a pretty good idea of what I wanted my life to look like, but I wasn't quite sure of how to get there. I wanted to be successful in real estate. That's a tall order without having a roadmap on how to get there. Most of my friends we either going to college, joining the military, hitting the corners, or going to work. I hadn't done too well informal educational settings, so college wasn't a good fit for me. Being as stubborn as I am would only land me in a stockade if I enlisted. My moral compass wouldn't let me work a corner, so entering the workplace was my only choice.

Planning for the Future

Getting a job was all well and good, but I still needed to make my job choices fit with and further my yet undefined long-term goals. I decided to work backward. If my ultimate goal was to own and develop enough real estate that I could live off that business, I would have to figure out how to purchase my first piece of property. Just out of high school, I didn't have a credit history, so I knew

I'd have to amass a hefty downpayment if I were to secure a mortgage. I would also have to make myself an attractive risk for a bank to invest in me.

A key metrics banks use in determining if you are a good risk is called a debt to equity ratio. Most financial terms sound like they would be difficult to understand, but they're not. You have to turn the terms into concepts that are familiar to you, and the rest is just numbers. Think of the debt to equity ratio as how much you have in credit card debt versus how much money you have in your bank account. If you have a lot more money in the bank versus the balance you have on your cards, you have a low debt to equity ratio, and someone might be willing to lend you more money. If your debt far exceeds the cash you can lay your hands on, no one is going to want to lend you a dime. It's a little more complicated than that, but the headline is low or no debt with a steady income makes you a better credit risk.

I had started listening to Dave Ramsey's radio show, and a low, or no, debt lifestyle is something he preaches. For those not familiar with Ramsey, he's a native Nashvillian with a commercial real estate background. Ramsey lost and found a number of fortunes and eventually became a financial advisor and talk radio show host. People call in during his show to ask for advice on their financial situations, and Ramsey fixes everything in thirty seconds or less.

While I don't agree with all of Ramsey's methods, two of his principles guide me. The first is what Ramsey calls the debt snowball. This is where someone starts paying off their debts, smallest to largest. Once the smallest debt is knocked out, what you were paying on the smallest debt is applied to the next largest debt. That continues until all of your debt is paid off. I didn't have any debt, but I figured I could do a reverse snowball to build my real estate empire. If I could buy one property and rent it out, then I could apply any profits from that property to purchase the next rental.

The second touchstone Ramsey uses is Proverbs 22:7 (King James Version), "The rich ruleth over the poor, and the borrower is servant to the lender." The point of wanting to own real estate was so I coud be my own boss. I didn't want to paint myself into a debt corner where I was struggling to make mortgage payments. I also didn't want to get myself in a situation where the value of the home is less than what the loan amount is. That's called being underwater on a loan, and it's not a good position to be in. A property can reduce in value for a number of reasons. For example, the local economy could tank, and the demand for housing could go down. This was a big concern in Columbia because of the city's fortunes being tied so closely to the Saturn plant. There had to be a way to minimize my risk and still go forward with my plans.

Buying My First Property

I then looked back at my family's example to show me the way forward. My grandfather had a solid plan on reducing his living expenses. I wasn't sold on living at a funeral home as something I wanted to do for free rent, so with my parents' blessings, I stayed at my parents' house. I wasn't trying to duck any responsibilities or not shoulder my load as an adult—they knew that. I was taking steps for a better future for myself. It was not much different than if I'd stayed home while taking classes at Columbia State. The difference was I'd be learning my lessons in the real world instead of in a classroom.

I wanted to go ahead and purchase my first property. I still had my job at McDonald's but wasn't making enough money to secure a loan. I quickly learned that the requirements for getting a commercial real estate loan are different than getting a mortgage for a house you're going to live in. The same principles apply to how banks evaluate commercial venture's creditworthiness as an individual. The difference is that some of the metrics are different for each type of loan. Also, there are some government loan guarantee programs, like the Federal Housing Administration (FHA), that can make getting a commercial loan a little easier.

No matter how I approached securing a loan, I didn't ring the right bells for the banks. I went to my father with a proposal. Some parents pay for their children to go to college in order to prepare them for a career. I wanted my father to do the same for me, but it wouldn't cost him a dime. All my father had to do was cosign on a loan for me. If was going to substitute the real world for a classroom, I would need his backing. I searched around Columbia for listings and found the perfect starter house. With my down payment, I would only have to take out a loan for $18,000. (This was in the early 2000s when real estate prices were much lower, especially in what was still considered rural Tennessee.)

My father heard my plan and agreed to cosign on the loan. A few weeks later, I was a homeowner. I put an ad in the paper to rent out the property, and it was not long before I had a tenant. I was an eighteen-year-old landlord without much backup. I had used most of my savings for the down payment. My tenant's rent covered the house note and let me with a little profit, but it was not enough to live on. If real estate was going to become a self-sustaining income for me, I would need to grow my empire. Expansion meant more income to buy more properties and have a cushion for maintenance and repair on my present rental property. I was ready for it and had my plan already in place.

Real estate can also be a highly profitable business model. Most people think about real estate in terms of flipping a property. That's where you buy a home or commercial property, fix it up, and then try to sell it. To make a profit, the property's sales price must be greater than the original purchase price, plus the renovation costs, and costs for the sale. Flipping requires a lot of upfront capital for a down payment on the property, material costs, and hiring contractors to do the renovations. The most successful flippers are contractors that have the skillset to do many of the renovations themselves. You can makes thousands of dollars on every flipped house you sell, but it's not a business model for beginners.

The advantage of purchasing rental property and being a landlord is that you have a steady stream of predictable income at a high profit margin. The margins from rental properties doesn't always come from the difference between the rent you charge versus your monthly loan payment and maintenance. The tax laws in the United States favor real estate ventures, so you can keep a higher percentage of what you make. Current tax laws allow you to deduct the interest you pay on a mortgage from your taxable income. You can also deduct depreciation expenses for both the house and any improvements you make on the property over a period of years. There are other tax incentives for purchasing and improving houses in historic and low-income neighborhoods. With all of these deductions you might be paying less in taxes for your real estate venture than you are at a nine-to-five gig. (Tax laws are always subject to change and you should consult a licensed tax professional in your state before entering any business venture)

I was armed with knowledge of the real estate market and the rest of my plan was unconventional. I decided to stay with McDonald's as my primary job. The company had been good to me since I was fifteen. I knew what I was doing, what to expect, and more importantly, I knew I wouldn't have to start over. Even though I wouldn't be leaving McDonald's, I was going to make some changes. I wasn't going to spend two or two-and-a-half hours commuting from Columbia to downtown Nashville. Time is too valuable a commodity to be spent stuck in Nashville traffic, so I started calling around to McDonald's locations closer to home. The Lord has a funny way of directing us where we need to go. There was a full-time opening at the restaurant in Brentwood.

Flipping Burgers in Brentwood

If Nashville has anything like Beverly Hills, it would be Brentwood. The area in south Nashville is a nexus of wealth and influence. To the northern border of the suburb are the multi-million dollar homes of Forest Hills. To the south lay old monied Antebellum estates of Franklin. My restaurant was a stone's throw from Brentwood's financial heart—Maryland Farms. The massive commercial real estate was once a horse farm owned by an entrepreneur named Truman Ward. It turns out that Ward knew land like he knew horses. His farm was less than a mile from I-65—close enough to be accessible with an exit ramp, but far enough away the constant hum of tractor-trailers would not disrupt a meeting. Through political backroom deals in the 1970s and '80s, Ward was able to get his 400-acre farm zoned commercially. The first building that went up was 30,000 square feet of class-A office space. The Brentwood Racket and Country Club was opened in Maryland Farms in 1978 and Andrews Cadillac soon followed.[2]

On the edge of Maryland Farms was the McDonalds I would be working at. Two country clubs and a few billion dollars in business were being transacted within a mile of my restaurant. I did not think it was possible, but the Brentwood McDonald's location was busier than the one at Vanderbilt. It was like every day was cheap burger Wednesday at the Brentwood location. I think, at one time or another, I probably saw every person that worked in Maryland Farms come to the golden arches. The Brentwood customers came for the same reasons the Vanderbilt hospital folks did—comfort. These chained to their cubicle workers needed a different kind of break than the stressed hospital crowd. You could tell by the way someone ordered that something had sucked the life out of their souls. It had to be their jobs, and I swore that would never be me.

The "Poor Man's" Country Club

The rhythms of Brentwood became second nature to me after being on the line a few months. When I was lucky enough to open up the store, I noticed a loose-knit group of men would have coffee together. You could tell they had not planned on meeting for coffee, but they all seemed to know each other and would chat whenever they saw each other. Most McDonald's restaurants have their groups of old retired folks that hold court over coffee and McGriddles. I didn't think much about these men until I started catching snippets of their conversations. These were rich old white guys, and their conversations always turned to how they made their money. There were retired stock-brokers, insurance men, a few real estate guys, and a dozen other business disciples that made up the informal coffee klatsch. Sitting at McDonald's made them feel like normal Joes.

When you listen, you can learn. At first, I would sweep up or wipe down tables around these guys. I well placed, "Good morning." or "How are you doing today?" was my version of getting my foot in the door. Then I would listen to what they said, understood what they were discussing, and then I started to talk to them. I told them about my dreams to own more real estate and to become financially independent. Once the prime movers of the group heard that, it was done. I was a kindred spirit, and they were more than happy to critique my plans. Much of the information they gave me was specifics about how to invest or how to limit my financial risk when investing. In general terms, they gave this advice:

- Always do what you are passionate about.
- Never go into personal debt if you do not have to.
- Live your life like you run a business. Keep your overhead low and find ways to increase your revenue.
- Only invest money that you can afford to lose.
- Unless you invest your earnings, you are never going to get rich working for someone else.

These were things that my family had taught me, but it was good to hear from people who had made enough money to retire comfortably. I could also tell that they lived the advice they were giving me. Most days, these guys were here at McDonald's instead of the Brentwood Country Club. A buck for a cup of coffee and good conversation was cheaper than a $40 breakfast at "the club." These retirees had all the money they would ever need, and McDonald's was their country club.

One of the McDonald's country club members was Johnny Fleeman. Johnny grew up in Lewisburg, Tennessee, a little town just down the road from Columbia. At the tender age of ten, Johnny pulled his little red wagon up and down the streets of Lewisburg looking for glass soda bottles. You could get a dime for turning in glass bottles to a grocery store. By the age of nineteen, Johnny bought a grocery store. Johnny would go on to be a restaurateur and sell his own line of specialty steak sauces. Johnny would always take the time to sit down with me and let me talk out my plans. He offered me ideas to help me along the way, but most importantly he validated that I was on the right track.

Johnny and his buddies' example helped me stick to my own plans. I was still living at home, driving an older model car, and living as lean as possible. Most of the things my friends were doing or buying, I held off on. I hardly ever went out to dinner or the movies. I did not have fancy clothes or jewelry. My frugal means didn't give me enough to start my real estate empire. The one thing I was not doing was finding additional ways to increase my revenue. I once again looked at my parents' and grandparents' examples and came up with long- and short-term solutions.

Working Two Jobs

Even as busy as the Brentwood McDonald's was, restaurant owners don't like to pay overtime unless absolutely necessary. If I did get a few hours of overtime here or there, it wasn't something I could count on. The easiest thing for me to do was to take a second job. If I was going to start buying more real estate, I would need to substantially beef up my income. I decided to stick with what I knew and approached a few fast food joints around McDonald's. The most promising lead I had was Back Yard Burgers. The micro-chain fast food joint first started selling burgers in a Cleveland, Mississippi grocery store during the late 1980s. Back Yard Burgers catered to those looking for a premium burger served in drive-thru times. The concept caught on a today the, now Nashville headquartered, company has more than thirty stores in the mid-South.

After a few discussions and applications, Back Yard Burgers offered me a full-time position. The markets were different enough that neither my bosses at McDonald's nor the manager at Back Yard Burger thought me working at both places would be a conflict of interest. Back Yard Burgers also never asked me for the recipe for McDonald's special sauce, so I was in there clear there. The main concern for my two employers was my ability to consistently keep up an eighty-hour workweek. I was eighteen or nineteen years old then, and my ambition was as limitless as my energy. I figured that within a couple of years, I would have enough money to put a down payment on purchasing a rental property. Hard work is one of the prerequisites for success, and I was ready to do my part.

A big advantage Brentwood Back Yard Burgers had for me was that it was literally across the street from McDonald's. At the end of my shift at McDonald's, I would head to the bathroom and change uniforms. There was not anywhere I could take a shower or freshen up between gigs. Many times, I was due to get off McDonald's at the same time I was supposed to punch in at Back Yard Burgers. The folks at Back Yard were understanding, but I would change lightning-quick and run across the street to make my start time.

There were days I drove the forty-five minutes home and it felt my eyeballs were covered in grease. Imagine the film you always wash from your kitchen cabinets every spring. That's a year's worth of vaporized oil and fat clinging to every surface in your kitchen. In either McDonalds or Back Yard Burger, we cooked more food in a day than most people cook in their kitchen during an entire year. I was constantly washing my uniforms because there is no wearing something for two days when you work fast food. It also felt like every couple of months, I was buying a new pair of shoes. Grease also breaks down the plastics used in shoes. One day you'd almost slip because the treads had invisibly worn away. The next pair of shoes you'd get seemed fine until mopping up at closing time. You'd get halfway done mopping the dining area's floor McDonald's and you'd realize your foot was wet. Dirty mop water seeped in through a tiny hole in the shoe's sole. A forty-five-minute drive with a mop water dirty sock feels like you are walking through a swamp.

Grease and physical fatigue are not the worst thing about working food service—it's the extremes. One minute you are standing over a hot grill or fryer and the next, you'd got to go to the freezer to retrieve stock. That's 100°F to -10°F in thirty seconds flat. Then there are the customers. You could take an order from the most pleasant person on the planet and the customer behind her you swore was sent from the devil to test your patience. Then a decent song would come on the radio that made you forget all of those troubles. That is until your manager told you to clean up the mess someone made in the bathroom. The extremes of working with the public would make you want to quit faster than dirty mop water socks or eighty-hour workweeks.

If all of those conditions weren't bad enough, working fast food can be damaging to your mental health. There were a small percentage of the Brentwood customers that wore elitism like a badge of honor. These problem customers seemed to go out of their way to make you feel like you were a deficient human because you worked fast food. I don't remember thousands of customers that I served over the years, but I remember the ones that tried to make me feel small and insignificant. It doesn't take many times hearing, "How simple can it be to flip a burger and you haven't even done that right," before you wonder if it's not true.

Worse than the defending yourself against customers bullying you was the threat of real danger in a fast food restaurant. At a traditional McDonald's location, life happens. Customers get together to share a meal. Divorced parents use the parking lot for a pickup/dropoff point for the kids. People meet to buy and sell items they have seen on Craigslist. In all these interactions, there is bound to be conflict. I have waded into my fair share of arguments and near fist fights to diffuse potentially explosive situations. It is never easy to mediate people who are seeing red, but for the good of the other customers and my crew, it occasionally had to be done.

There is the one nightmare scenario that you hope that never will happen—an armed robbery. In the early 2000s, many fast food restaurants were still cash-only businesses. Even after McDonald's started accepting debit cards, most customers still paid cash. The lure of a quick cash payday has always made lunchtime at a fast food restaurant an attractive target for crooks. I never thought an armed robbery would happen at the Brentwood location. The restaurant is far enough from the interstate that a fast getaway would not make it an attractive target. Evidently the guy that held up my store skipped that day in criminal school.

Getting robbed is everything you would expect it to be and a few things you don't. Time doesn't slow down, and you don't see you life flash before your eyes. What does happen is panic. Every muscle in your body wants to move. It does not matter where you go as long as it's away from the robber. You fight your own mind and body to stay put, because if you don't, bad things are sure to happen to other people. So you stand, empty the cash drawer, and pray you'll live to see the next day. Lucky for me and everyone in the restaurant, the robber was out as quick as he came in. After it was all over, I wondered if I should quit and go into a different line of work.

Quitting was not an option. Some criminal wasn't going to take away my dreams by scaring me off my path. I revisited the basics and remined myself of what I had in sight because all of this was temporary. Working two full-time jobs was only the short-term portion of my plan. The long-term piece was to move up the ladder at McDonald's. Back Yard

Burgers is a fine company to work for, but there are many fish in a small pond. Back Yard Burgers treated their employees well enough that management teams tended to be there for long periods of time. With McDonald's, management positions turned over more quickly. Management talent was moved around where it was needed. there were always problems at one location, vacations to be filled, or someone taking a leave of absence that required the shuffling of management. This was true of both McDonald's franchise and corporate restaurants. What all of that meant for me was opportunity. I have heard it said that "Luck is what happens when preparation meets opportunity." I like to think luck has an element of the divine in it, but the rest of the statement is absolutely a recipe for success.

Mr. D

When I was at the Vanderbilt McDonald's, I tried to learn everything I could informally. There were thousands of combinations of employees, food, and equipment that have to go correctly for every burger and fry combo that went out the door. When I didn't know how to do something, I'd watch to see how that was done. I'd ask questions if I didn't understand what was going on. Then I would try to do it on my own. If I messed it up, I'd do it over until I got it right. If you boil down my success at anything, it follows that pattern—observe/learn, ask questions, and try it on your own until you get it right.

After a year of working at both McDonald's and Back Yard Burgers, I was still standing. Days off were few and far between, but I was growing my bank account. I'm sure that the management teams at both Back Yard Burgers and McDonald's were both surprised at how I did it. Many of my co-workers would call out for no good reason, but not me. Day after day, I would be there. The word of my marathon run at two jobs reached the ear of my restaurant's franchise owner, James Daughtry. When he came into the store, you quickly learned never to call him Mr. Daughtry. When he was in one of his restaurants, he was simply Mr. D. He treated everyone that worked for him with the respect of a father. He was quick to point out a restaurant's deficiencies but was never mean-spirited. He simply expected his restaurants to run cleanly and efficiently. And that's what we gave him.

The seemingly informal leadership style of Mr. D came from a man who had been working where his employees were. Mr. D was a black man who had started out as a McDonald's janitor. He worked his way through North Carolina Agricultural and Technical State University. He graduated there in 1973 with honors and a degree in business administration. Mr. D worked for McDonald's for twenty-two years and became a McDonald's franchise owner in 2001. He would go on to own twelve McDonald's franchises under The Good Food Group corporation. On top of all that, I knew from speaking to Mr. D he was involved with flipping real estate. That is where someone buys a run-down property, fixes it up, and resells it for a profit. I do not believe Mr. D ever did anything that didn't turn to gold. He was the most successful black man I had ever met, and I had a tremendous amount of respect for him.

One day Mr. D came into the store for an unscheduled visit. He made the rounds with the staff and did a cursory inspection of the restaurant. He was almost done with his tour and hadn't said anything to me yet. I had been busy taking care of customers, but I thought it was odd he didn't say anything to me. I thought he might have even left when I heard Mr. D say, "James, do you have a minute?"

You always had a minute for Mr. D when he came into the store. I finished up what I was doing and went over to him standing in the dining area. He looked at me and said, "I hear you're working another full-time job on top of this one."

I didn't know what was going on. There was not any use in lying about it—not that hiding the truth was the right thing to do anyway. Everyone in the restaurant and at Back Yard Burgers across the street knew what I was doing. I looked Mr. D in the eye and said, "Yes, sir. I am."

"And you're not missing any work here, and you believe you're performing your job duties here satisfactorily," Mr. D further probed.

Was I not pulling my weight during my shifts here? Did I forget to do something? Were their customer complaints? Did I fall asleep behind the cash register and did not realize it? I could not think of anything that I had done or not done to make Mr. D drop the hammer on me. So, I said, "No, sir. I don't miss work and I do my job."

Mr. D started to smile and said, "Yes, James. You certainly do your job and then some. I'd like to make you a shift manager."

Here I thought I was in trouble, but I got a promotion out of the deal. I happily accepted Mr.

D's offer and became his newest shift manager. I thought I'd worked hard before, but I was really going to have to step up my game now if I was going to lead a crew. I also began to understand that the people I surrounded myself with mattered. Everyone I came in contact with was helping me along the way—the morning coffee guys, Mr. D, and even the rest of my crew were serving as an example to me.

The Benefits of Learning Spanish

There was a group of Hispanics that worked in my restaurant. Some of them spoke little or no English, but that didn't stop them from doing a top-notch job. They had a work ethic and sense of community, even in the restaurant, that strengthened their individual job performances. I decided that if I was going to be a leader, then I needed to learn how to communicate with everyone on my crew. My resolve to become bilingual was strengthened by a young lady I worked with who spoke mostly Spanish. I wanted to ask her out for a date, but I wanted to do so in Spanish.

I began learning Spanish the same way I had done everything else—by listening, asking questions, and trying it myself. I had already picked up a few phrases of the language here and there. It's impossible to work in close proximity with someone speaking a different language and not pick up on something. When I heard a Spanish word I thought meant something, take a cup, for instance, I would say the word and hold up a cup. I would do the same for verbs and acted out an activity while saying the word. After getting more confident in my vocabulary, I tried my hand at sentences. Sometimes my attempts were met with giggles from the Spanish-speaking crew. My version of saying, "Could you hand me the saltshaker" to them sounded more like, "I have worms coming out of my ears."

One day I was helping sweep up the dining area with one of my Spanish-speaking colleagues. I was trying to communicate in Spanish and probably was doing a poor job of it. One of the customers seated at a booth asked me if I was learning to speak Spanish. I explained that I was and why I felt it necessary to communicate with my crew. I think I might have even admitted that another motivation was to get a date. The customer paid more attention to my story than simply making idle chit-chat. When I finished my explanation, he told me that he was a reporter for the *Tennessean*—Nashville's main newspaper. He told me that my trying to learn Spanish was a story people needed to hear about. At the time, there was a public debate about whether or not government documents should be English only or English should be adopted as the official language of the United States. The reporter felt that stories of people building language bridges, like me, would help put those debates into perspective.

I was floored by the reporter's offer. I couldn't imagine that someone would want to hear about me fumbling through Spanish sentences, but I agreed to an interview. It was a little challenging getting our schedules straight, but I sat down with the reporter on one of my days off. He asked me background questions, and somehow, the conversation got around to me owning rental property. The tables were turned on the reporter and it was his turn to be surprised at a nineteen-year-old landlord who worked two jobs. The focus of his story dramatically shifted. He wanted to know everything about how I had gotten interested in real estate to how I purchased the property.

The reporter wanted to mention that I worked for McDonald's, but I was not sure about that. There were strict policies about McDonald's employees speaking to the media, and I had no interest in losing my job. After the interview was over, I spoke with my bosses about the piece. Evidently, the folks at McDonald's corporate did not want to mention me working there in the article. I never found out why they would object to being associated with me in this context. I approached my manager at Back Yard Burgers, and he made a call to the corporate office. Back Yard Burgers was more than happy to let the world know I was a future bilingual real estate mogul.

I thought it would be cool to see my story in print. I'd buy dozens of copies of the newspaper to give out to my family and friends. One of my friends would tease me about being a superstar for a couple of weeks, and that would be the extent of my fifteen minutes of fame. There are many things in my life I have been right about, but I could not have been more wrong about the reaction to this article.

Getting Ink

The *Tennessean* is an evening delivery newspaper and is circulated to thirty-nine counties in Middle Tennessee and eight bordering Kentucky counties. The morning after the story about me dropped, it seemed like everyone who came to McDonald's knew my name and story. People came up to me and wanted to congratulate me on the piece. Some people even asked me for advice about real estate or how I was able to hold down two jobs while being a landlord. For the next week or so, women would come into either McDonald's or Back Yard Burgers and ask me on dates. I was also getting contacted by real estate companies who were offering me jobs. All this from a guy who did not graduate high school and was just trying to make his way in the world.

I turned down most of the inquiries about jobs and dates. I did not think my family would have approved of someone of the women who wanted to go out, and I did not like many of the job offers. Most of the employment opportunities I received felt like they wanted me as an administrative assistant. Their pitches were full of platitudes like, "Kid, you can get your foot in the door until you learn the ropes." Those offers sounded like they would use me for a couple of years and trade on the good publicity I'd received in the *Tennessean* article.

There was one real estate company offer that was different. The company's owner sounded like he wanted to help me develop as a businessman and entrepreneur. I was cautiously optimistic about the offer when I went to the firm's office. The space was clean, and the deco was trendy. When I investigated the realtors' offices, they all had "I love me" walls—artfully arranged certificates of achievement, pictures of happy clients, and *National Geographic* quality vacation photos. Everything was placed to make clients feel like their realtor was successful and therefore the best choice to buy or sell your property.

I spoke with the owner for a bit, and he seemed like a nice enough guy. There was not anything sinister about him, but I felt like I had been taken up to the pinnacle of the Temple and was shown the world below me. Don't get me wrong, he was no devil, but his offer would have taken my soul. I saw a future that I did not want. There would be licenses and certifications I would have to get. Someone would take me out and I would get some nice suits and a car that would impress clients. I'd have to go to dinner parties and social events talking to people about things that didn't interest me just to get their business. With that kind of backing, it would be easier for me to become a rich man.

That life wasn't what I wanted. I wanted to make it on my terms. Even though I worked eighty-plus hours a week at fast food, that was my choice. I had the flexibility to make whatever moves on the real estate market I wanted. If I took this job, I'd probably work just as much and at the end of the day, I wouldn't have achieved my goals. No, I was going to do this my way because I had a vision and faith.

The owner had taken me into his office and explained how he saw my future with the company. It was close to what I had envisioned. He went through some of their current projects and the company's history too. At the end of his presentation, he asked me, "What do you think?"

"I appreciate your offer, but I don't think it's for me," I replied.

When I left his office, I picked up a copy of the *Tennessean* and looked for the real estate listings. I had enough money in the bank, and it was about time for me to buy another house.

Chapter Three
Learning Hard Lessons

I try to never look back and wonder "what if" at the decisions I have made in my life. We can all remember the crossroads in our lives that have happened. You can spend sleepless nights wondering what would have happened if you had gone another way. I did not do that after the job offers that resulted from the publication of the *Tennessean* article. I also did not lay awake wondering what future crossroads I would come to. Even if I had looked ahead, I would not have been able to foresee what crossroads I would come to.

The Real Estate Snowball

By the time I was twenty-one, I owned six rental properties. My plan of using Dave Ramsey's debt snowball in reverse to buy properties was working. On an average of every six months, I bought a new property. I applied all the profit from my other rental properties and what I had saved from my two jobs to a down payment for my latest acquisition. To make the math easy, let's say I needed a $10,000 down payment to secure a property. Each rental property clears $500 per month profit and I could kick in another $500 from my fast-food jobs earnings. That means that it would take me ten months to save up the down payment for property number two. With two properties, I could save $1,500 a month, and purchasing the next property would take seven months. Three properties and my fast food paycheck would net $2,000 a month and would take five months to secure a down payment for property number four.

Purchasing each successive property became easier from a credit perspective too. Each month I paid the mortgage on a house, I had more equity in that property. Think of equity as a percentage of ownership you have on a home. Once again, to simplify the math, say you've taken a $100,000 loan on a home. After you have repaid $1,000 of the mortgage, you own 1 percent of that house. That 1 percent is referred to in financial terms as equity.[3] The more equity and property I had made me a better credit risk for banks to lend to me. A client with a lower credit risk also gets better interest rates on loans. If I had a lower interest rate on successive properties, I would profit more per month than my earlier purchased properties.

Thinking about piles of cash being mailed to you every month is the glamourous side of owning real estate. You don't feel like a rock star when one of your tenants calls with busted pipes at 2 AM. Evicting a tenant is a long and costly process that doesn't make a landlord any friends. Tenants are also rough on rental properties because they don't own the place. The good news is that these situations are the minority. Most people pay their rent and take pride in having a decent place to live.

If landlords expect their tenants to pay rent and treat the property with respect, a tenant has expectations for the landlord. A renter has the right to expect a decent and safe place to live at an affordable price. That means that if you plan on being an ethical landlord, you have got to reinvest in your properties. No one wants to live in a house with carpet that has been there since Ronald Reagan was president, so you must periodically update the interiors to fit current housing trends. A wise landlord will also have his or her own periodic maintenance schedule that includes inspection of appliances, HVAC units, the roof, and the foundation. Catching problems early not only buys you goodwill from your clients, but it also increases your profitability.

If you know how to do basic home maintenance, you can save yourself a ton of profit dollars. How much does it cost to fix a leaky faucet? With the right know-how, it could be a few minutes of your time and less than $5 in materials. Calling a plumber could be a $75 call-out fee, plus time spent on the repair, plus materials. More importantly, fixing that faucet shows your tenant that you care about their wellbeing. If your focus isn't on providing a decent place for someone else to live, you should probably check out another way to make money.

It turns out that I had quite a few people start asking me how to make money. I'd get stopped by someone while I was on break at McDonald's or when I was out and about. I heard some outlandish ideas about how to make money. Sadly, I heard many misconceptions about how money works. I began to understand that in my community, the fundamentals of money management were largely a mystery. Money was something that when you had it, you spent it. When what money you had runs low, you scraped by or borrowed to make it to the next payday. The concept of budgeting was as foreign as the Greek language to the people I spoke with. That needed to change.

Mo' Money Mondays

I can't remember how we connected, but during this time, Trent Overton was put in my orbit. Trent hosted a radio show about money matters on a local radio station. He asked me to appear on the show for a segment and the on-air chemistry worked with us. I was soon asked to be a regular guest on his show. We called the show *Mo' Money Mondays* and I was aiming to be a black Dave Ramsey. The *Mo' Money Mondays* format was similar to *The Davy Ramsey Show*. We talked about some financial matters at the beginning of the show and then took calls.

I was on the air around 2005–6 just before the financial crisis of 2007–8. If I had the eyes to see it,

I would have known a financial storm was brewing on the horizon from the calls we received. You would expect calls regarding how to stretch dollars and make ends meet on a show like this, but the circumstances were different. People were experiencing financial difficulties through no fault of their own and they didn't understand why.

To understand what was going on in the early 2000s, let's look at some national averages around the time *Mo' Money Mondays* was on the air. The minimum wage in the United States was $5.15 in 2004–6.[4] During that same time period, a gallon of gas went from $1.88 to $2.59—that's almost a 38 percent increase.[5] A gallon of milk went from $2.78 to $3.20—a 15 percent increase.[6] In 2005, the average wage increase was 3.66 percent.[7] All of that means that if you were an average American, your wages weren't keeping up with the cost of living. No matter how much budgeting you did or how financially responsible you were, you were likely to have to adjust your lifestyle to accommodate life's necessities.

Fielding calls from people who want to work but suddenly find it hard to fill their gas tanks up to get to work is difficult. We had a couple of minutes to listen to someone's problem and try and suggest a solution. Many times, the only solution we had was to tell someone to pick up a side hustle. I was a twenty-three years old, working two jobs, landlord of six rental properties, and a radio show host. It was easy to tell a single mother with two kids to buck up and get another job. In fact, there were not (and still aren't) many other solutions. The rising cost of living and the company's unwillingness to pay workers a living wage necessitate hard decisions. Many times, the only option someone has to rise above their circumstances is working more and sleeping less.

My personal successes made me feel like I needed to rise above my daily grind. I mentioned that I was never one to feel the need to go out to dinner or to a club, but as I approached my mid-twenties, those things changed. I think there's a certain amount of folly we must experience in our youth to get it out of our systems. I'm not talking about anything scandalous, but you have to try different things to appreciate a quiet night at home. I started to dip my toe in the waters of the world. I had sushi for the first time. I went to a nightclub or two with my friends. I'd ask a girl out and spend a little too much on the date. My wardrobe was in bad need of an overhaul, so I got new clothes.

None of the behaviors I was exhibiting were necessarily bad. What was detrimental was that I was deviating from my plan. I felt like I deserved the fruits of my labor even though I had not achieved all my goals. Spending more money on a lifestyle meant that I had less money to buy more property. So I slowed my roll on property acquisitions a little. I could take a little break and have a little fun. All my properties paid for themselves, and I had enough financial cushion for any unexpected expenses. So, what's the problem with all of that?

Looking back to that time, I should have stuck to my plan. There is nothing wrong with taking a short breather or giving yourself an occasional indulgence. The problem comes in when you do not have the discipline to go back to your original plan after treating yourself. I now believe that being successful isn't only about flowing through with a good plan. Being successful is about keeping momentum while you're executing a good plan. Momentum is the key to success for anything from real estate to exercise plans. When you press pause on your plan, for any reason, it takes more effort to get back into a groove than it does to keep executing your daily plan. The danger is that you will get used to the ease that not sticking to your plan gives you, and you will never get back on track.

The other danger of getting off track is that you will make poor decisions making up for lost time. Let's say you have been regularly investing $50 a week in a mutual fund. You decide you will stop investing for a couple of months and use that money to live a little. You use the money you should have been investing to eat out a couple of times a week. After a couple of months of take out, you come to the realization you need to get back to inventing.

You have got nothing to show for all those dinners out. You've not really saved that much time for the convenience of having someone else cook for you. You decide that for the next couple of months, there will be no dinners out and you will not spend money on anything. That means pushing back getting new tires for your car or turning the thermostat down ten degrees in the winter to save a few bucks. You will have the money to replace the lost investment funds in no time, but at what cost to your comfort and personal safety?

Carver House

My version of getting back on track was to find a bigger real estate venture to get involved with. That came in the form of the Carver House in Columbia. This sixty-unit apartment complex had nothing going for it. The apartments were ground zero for the drug trade in Columbia. You could get any illegal substance you wanted by walking into the parking lot of Carver House. To facilitate the drug trade, the pushers shot out the streetlights on the block around the complex and in the parking lot. Any time day or night, you would see kids patrolling the sidewalks as lookouts. If they saw the police or anyone who looked like they might be the cops, they would whistle a few times. At that sound, everyone standing outside Carver House would scatter.

If you did make it past the lookouts, the marketplace was open to you. Each dealer had a different setup, but the principles were the same. You would place your order with one of the dealers and give him your money. Then you would go to an apartment where the drugs would be given to you through a slot in the door. The other variation was that someone other than the dealer, usually a juvenile called a runner, would bring the drugs out to you from a central stash. The dealer never touched money and the drugs at the same time. In theory, if the dealer were arrested, he could claim the money was for a lamp or sofa he had just sold the buyer. The runner held a small enough quantity of drugs the cops could only charge them with simple possession. If that runner were under eighteen, they would get a slap-on-the-wrist juvenile charge.

I could have picked other properties to set my sights on that had less baggage. Rumor had it that the ownership of Carver House had once belonged to the County. It was seized for back property taxes, or for some other reason, and sold for a dollar at auction. I wasn't sure if that story was true, but I did know the property was presently for sale for quite a bit more than a dollar. I just had to figure out how to purchase it.

One of the things my grandfather had taught me was to deal with local banks whenever possible. A financial institution with a stake in the community and knows the people they are dealing with will be more likely to give you a loan. It's hard to turn down a loan when you're dealing with someone that dated your Aunt Hattie or who went to school with your parents. I had always used one of the banks in Columbia for my other real estate purchases and scheduled an appointment to discuss a loan for Carver House.

When the day came, I was ready for the appointment. I had projections for how much it would cost to renovate the property and my expected income. I had plans on top of plans for Carter House and was excited to tell my banker what they would be buying into. When I sat down at the loan officer's desk, I could tell this would be a hard sell. He had a look on his face like he had been sucking on a sour Jawbreaker. He greeted me and asked in his slow Southern drawl, "Now, why would you want to go and buy Carver House, James?"

He did not say that maliciously. I took it more like a good friend asking you if you really wanted to swim in a pond filled with water moccasins. My reasons were plentiful, and I explained myself as best I could. First, low-income does not mean that you do not deserve dignity. The legitimate folks that lived in Carter House needed a clean and safe place to live. Secondly, I knew I could make money with Carver House. I had recently read *Trump: The Art of the Deal* and some of the points had stuck with me.

Think what you want about the former president, but Donald Trump's success in real estate is impressive. *Trump: The Art of the Deal* made me reevaluate my real estate plan. In Trump's book, he said, "Most people think small because they are afraid of success, afraid of making decisions, afraid of winning."[8] My real estate purchases had been limited to single-family dwellings and duplexes. I had gotten good at managing those types of properties and was comfortable with those types of properties. Growth does not happen when you're comfortable. If I was going to truly make it big in real estate, I needed to move on to more challenging projects. And if nothing else, Carter House was a challenge.

One of those challenges my banker asked me about was drug trafficking. It wasn't a secret in Columbia what went on in Carver House. The truth was I didn't have much of a plan to clear the drug dealers out. I already knew they would leave. I knew quite a few of the guys dealing from Carver House. I had either gone to school with them, or they knew my uncle who used to work the corners. One of the times I'd gone over to Carver House, I met with a few dealers to tell them I was thinking about buying the property.

The dealers were all for the idea of me buying Carver House, even though they knew what it would mean. They were not immune to the subtle gentrification of downtown Columbia, and they were smart. If you had the idea that they would fight to keep their turf, like Hollywood presents when this situation happens, you'd be wrong. When gentrification happens in any area, that means someone with money is pulling strings. Big money means the local government is going to protect the investment in the community. That means more cops making busts to send the message this area is now off-limits. Like I said, dealers are smart. The last thing they want is heat from the police. When renovation crews start rolling in, the dealers move their operation to the next block. Staying out of sight opened new markets for the dealers. Hipsters score too, you know.

The conversations I had with the Carver House dealers did take an unexpected turn. They would rather Carver House be owned by someone they knew, instead of a conglomerate out of Nashville or China. The longer we talked, the more they asked how I had gotten into a position where buying Carver House was an option. These hardcore bangers started to pick my brain about real estate. Why not? Who wants to be in that game forever? They had access to cash for down payments too.

Years later, I would find out that some of them did start buying real estate and got out of the life. That was one of the few good things that came out of my experience with Carver House.

The loan officer was unimpressed with my self-policing promises of clearing drugs out of Carver House. There were a few legal issues that could happen that would make underwriting a mortgage on that property riskier than my previous purchases. The local government could, at any time, condemn Carver House for being a public nuisance. Even though my plan was to turn that around, it would not happen overnight. All it would take was a few high-profile crimes at Carver House, and there goes the bank's money. The other consideration was federal forfeiture laws. The Feds can seize assets connected with the sale of drugs. Usually, these forfeiture laws are for property bought with drug money. There have been cases where a renter has been busted for distribution of drugs and the landlord's property has been seized.

Without a substantially greater cash down payment to offset the bank's risk, I would not be receiving the Carter House loan. I left the bank a little dejected but determined that I would get the project off the ground. I had a gentleman by the name of Raj who had been hounding me to buy one of my rental properties. I wasn't quite sure why he wanted it so badly. It was a simple rental house in an average Columbia neighborhood. It was one of the first properties I purchased and selling it would have netted me a $10,000 profit. I decided to call Raj up and discuss selling. Maybe I could turn the profit into something that would help me buy the Carver House.

Another reason I was considering selling to Raj was I felt we were cut from the same cloth. Raj was originally from New Delhi, India, and had immigrated to the United States with seven dollars in his pocket. He started working as a janitor and parlayed his earnings into a descent sized real estate empire. Raj was one of those fellows that also had his finger on construction and retail ventures. If there was money to be made, Raj was there in the thick of it.

While Raj and I were discussing the house's sale, I told him about my plans to purchase Carver House and the bank's resistance to giving me a loan. Raj instantly became intrigued about the prospects of owning the apartment complex. He wanted to hear more about my plan, but he had a condition. This should have triggered an alarm bell, but somehow it didn't. Raj said that he would be ostracized by his fellow Indians if they knew he was doing business with a black man. We would have to meet at a Waffle House outside of town to discuss business. I understood his concerns. I have seen my share of racism throughout my life and didn't want him to go through it anymore.

We met later that week at the Waffle House and hatched plans to purchase Carver House. Raj had the collateral and credit to be the face of the purchase. I could supply money for the down payment to buy-in to the project I had just brought to him. He said that we could be a 51/49 percent partners in the venture. I would run the day-to-day operations of the renovations while Raj worried about more strategic matters. He would use his connections to secure contractors and cheaper materials for Carver House's facelift. The split and division of labor sounded like a good deal. I wouldn't have 1 percent of Carver House without Raj, so I agreed to his terms.

There were more late-night meetings at Waffle House over the next few weeks. He kept me in the loop about how the loan process was going, and I stayed a silent partner for the moment. We almost lost the property after its first inspection. Carver

House was structurally sound, but it had mold. This wasn't the type of mold that a little Clorox will take care of. This was the type of mold that guys in hazmat suits come in to clean up. Raj told me there was nothing to worry about. Somehow Raj made the mold problem go away. To this day, I don't know how Raj made that happen. Whatever he did, the loan went through, and we bought Carver House.

Over the next few months of our partnership, more mold-like problems cropped up. Raj became predictable in his turn of phrase. Repeatedly I'd hear Raj say, "It's no problem. There's nothing to worry about. It's just a misunderstanding. I'll sort it out." I should have listened to that little voice inside my head after the first time.

My favorite example of Raj taking care of things was about halfway through the renovations. Since I was the operations manager of the Carver House renovation, I had to check in daily to direct and inspect the work crews. This is on top of the eighty hours a week I worked at my two fast-food jobs. Inevitably there would be problems crop up that had nothing to do with the Carver House structure. The work crews were not getting paid on time. Foremen would tell me that their line of credit had run dry at building supply stores. One of the stoppages was so severe that I had to go to Raj's office to sort it out. The crew was threatening to walk off and find other work if they did not get paid. Raj was furious when I told him the news. I wasn't sure if Raj was mad at me for coming to his office or for the crew threatening to walk off. Whatever the reason, Raj's stress management tool was repeatedly kicking a refrigerator.

"It's no problem. There's nothing to worry about. It's a misunderstanding. I'll sort it out."

That wasn't the last time I heard Raj use these phrases. As frustrated as I got with the renovations' rough going, Raj eventually did make everything alright. He made everything so right that when we were almost done updating Carver House, Columbia's daily newspaper the *Daily Herald* caught wind of the story. They interviewed Raj about what he had accomplished. There was a picture in the paper of him at the property. I might have been mentioned as a footnote, but it was clear who the hero was—Raj. I could not be publicly seen as having anything to do with the project because it might hurt his community's standing. That hurt, but at least the tenants of Carver House would have a good home.

In the months that came after the newspaper article, issues at Carver House calmed. I was naive to assume I would be able to check in on Carver House from time-to-time and collect my end of the rent. Raj called me one day and wanted to have a meeting. This was at the hour before the dawn of the 2007–8 financial crisis. There were rumors of real estate ventures hitting hard times, but rumors abound in the real estate world. When I got to the Waffle House, Raj was already there looking like he had just lost a puppy. He told me that some of his other business ventures were faltering. If something didn't change soon, he would have to file for bankruptcy within the month.

I was floored.

I did not have the capital to buy out Raj's 51 percent interest in Carver House. If he filed for bankruptcy, all his assets would be tied up in court proceedings possibly for years. My claim on any income from Carver House would not matter to a bankruptcy court. If Raj had liens on other property or creditors, the courts would pay them long before I would see a dime. Raj did have a suggestion. He could pay me $20,000 in cash now to buy out my end of Carver House. That way I would get something for my effort and not be caught up in the mess that was about to happen.

I accepted.

I supposed something was better than nothing. My time with Raj had been more of a pain than anything, so I chalked the loss up to experience. I could take my buyout money and purchase another rental house. That is what I was comfortable with. Maybe I should have stayed in my lane and not tried for anything better. Maybe.

A few weeks went past, and I was at my bank conducting some business or the other. The loan officer that had turned me down walked up to me and patted me on the back. He then proceeded to congratulate me on the sale of Carver House. I was confused. I hadn't told anyone that Raj had bought me out, let alone the circumstances of the sale. That was Raj's business and I'd dodged a bullet, so there was no reason to gossip.

I must have looked like someone had hit me with a catfish because the loan officer said, "Carver House. It just sold for $1.5 million."

I did not know what to do. I could hardly breathe. I understood the words he had just said, but I could not process them. I had a good idea of what the profit from that sale would have been, and 49 percent of the profit was way more than the $20,000 I had received. I made my apologies to the loan officer and drove straight to Raj's office. I did not care who saw me or if he broke his foot kicking his refrigerator. I was going to get some answers.

To my surprise, Raj let me in and asked me to sit down. I could tell that he knew exactly why I was there. I am sure he had been planning on this moment since he made the sale. I didn't say a word and tried to get my emotions reined in before opening my mouth. I did not have to say anything because Raj spoke first.

"I did you a favor, you know."

Favor? Did me a favor? I still couldn't speak, but Raj went on.

"You should never trust anyone in business. Now, you will think twice before getting into business with someone else. See—I did you a favor."

I walked out of his office without anything else to say. Son of a…

Chapter Four
Taking a Risk

Raj was right. He taught me a lesson that I did not think I'd have to learn—at least not from a fellow businessman. Even the drug dealers at Carver House had a code they lived by. If you did not cross them, you would get exactly what you paid for. Dave Ramsey calls experiences like mine "a stupid tax." I should have protected myself better on the front end and walked away when I saw the warning signs. A deal is only good if it is good for everyone, and it hadn't been good for me since jump street. The entire ordeal left me wondering if I should even be in the real estate business.

Raj's betrayal shook me on a spiritual level as well. I had always gone to church as a young man. When I was in high school, I would go with my buddy James to his Pentecostal church. There was something about those who gathered at James's church that was electric. You felt the spirit in every word and movement they made. From the time I left high school to a year or so before the Raj incident, I must admit my church attendance was lacking. I considered myself a believer, but the church was not a priority in my life.

My Sister

My younger sister changed all of that. She had a sweet disposition and a faith any of us would be proud to have. Many of the faithful, like my sister, are saddled with a thorn in the flesh like the Apostle Paul. In some ways, she followed along in Paul's footsteps as Galatians 4:13–14 says:

> You know that because of physical infirmity I preached the gospel to you at the first. And my trial which was in my flesh you did not despise or reject, but you received me as an angel of God, *even* as Christ Jesus.

My sister preached to me even though she never did so from a podium. My sister preached to me with her unending faith.

Her thorn in the flesh was a seizure disorder. She had a bad reaction to a medication when she was a toddler that caused the disorder. There was no trigger to the seizures my parents could ever figure out, the seizures happened when they happened. It was not like flashing lights or eating certain foods gave her a fit. One minute she was fine—then it happened. Sometimes she would get a blank stare for a few minutes and then be fine. Other times, the thousand-yard stare would be the precursor to a seizure.

Her entire life, she had this disorder, but she also had faith in God. She read her Bible. She prayed without ceasing. She sang. And my sister's faith never allowed her to believe God never makes mistakes. For whatever reason He saw fit to saddle her with this thorn, she accepted it.

I don't know if I could have been as forgiving as my sister. Many people would have cursed God for going through what she did. She would never be able to get a driver's license because of the disorder. She'd never hike alone in the woods for fear of an episode causing her to fall down. There were a thousand other "normal" activities that were out of her reach. That my sister kept on believing was her perpetual sermon to me.

My sister had a seizure bad enough she had to be hospitalized when she was eighteen. The situation was dire enough that I cannot remember all of the details. Between trying to care for my parents and feeling helpless to do anything to help my sister, memories of that time are sparse. I remember we all prayed over her for days. I remember that at one point, my sister's heart had stopped and she was technically dead. The hospital staff started her heart back after a minute or two on the other side. When she regained consciousness, she just said, "Thank you, Jesus."

I don't know what, if anything, she saw during those few minutes. Maybe her spirit had not yet left her body, and she didn't have the chance to see beyond. She would have that chance shortly after when God called my sister home. She passed on Super Bowl XXXIX Sunday. The Eagles were playing the Patriots that year. Every Super Bowl Sunday makes me think of her. I was baptized a week after my sister died. There could not have been a more impactful person in my life than my sister. I have no doubt that one of her purposes in life was to show me the way. Thank you.

Getting Back on the Horse

It was in the infancy of my faith that the Raj situation happened. I cannot say that I wasn't a little salty about the whole affair, but I tried not to let the actions of a man shake my faith in the Almighty. I prayed for guidance for what my next business move needed to be. The answer came to me, oddly enough, while driving around Carver House.

One of my goals with Carver House had been to give the neighborhood some hope. I knew that it was impossible to clear away all the issues that made Carver House into a drug palace with a fresh coat of paint. Carver House was meant to be a symbol for the community that positive change is possible. I had played my part in Carver House, but now it was time for me to get out of my slump and do more good for the community.

Within a few blocks of Carver House were crack houses and shooting galleries. These homes were flophouses where someone could purchase and smoke a crack rock or inject a hit of heroin into one's veins. The attraction for addicts was they could get their fix while being in the company of fellow addicts. It was their version of going to a local bar after work. There were no judgments to your actions, and someone could do as they pleased.

The owners of the crack houses and shooting galleries were profiting as much as the dealers. Most crack houses started out as low-end rental properties that were a few years away from needing major renovations. It is cheaper to let a property spiral into disrepair while exacting full rent than it is to fix the place up. The landlords of the crack houses were as complicit in selling drugs as the dealers themselves. It also only takes one or two crack houses to tarnish a neighborhood. These properties spread hopelessness through an entire community. I began to hatch a plan that would get me back into the real estate game and help my community.

Remember that all of this was happening before the financial crisis of 2007–8. Back then, mortgages were easy to come by. After the September 11th attacks on the World Trade Center and Pentagon, the United States economy nearly ground to a halt. The Federal Reserve reduced the interest rate they lend money to banks to nearly nothing. The thought was that if banks could borrow money at a reduced rate, the public would benefit from lower-cost loans. The lower rates weren't just tied to mortgages. Cheap money was out there for everything from starting new businesses to car loans. The theory was that lower interest rates stimulate the economy. That worked for a few years, but there were unintended consequences that diverged to crash the economy. I would become a victim of one of the unintended consequences.

To understand what happened to me and the economy around 2007, you first must understand real estate finance. Going out and getting a home loan might seem as simple as a bank giving you a pile of cash and expecting to get paid back with interest. There is nothing simple that happens with the background of a mortgage. Ninety percent of America's mortgages are backed by one of two government-sponsored agencies called Fannie Mae and Freddie Mac.[9] Fannie Mae and Freddie Mac buy mortgages after they are issued by your bank. This allows banks to recuperate funds from big mortgage payouts and issue more mortgages quicker. Because of Fannie Mae and Freddie Mac's backing, banks reduce the risk of issuing home loans. This gives stability to the mortgage market and allows some people to purchase a home where otherwise they might not have been able to.

Fannie Mae and Freddie Mac can sell off the mortgages they have bought to other financial institutions. Buying and selling debt sounds like a fairy tale, but it is how financial markets work on everything from mortgages to medical bills. Here is how it happens. Say your buddy Tim is running short until payday and he needs $100 to make it through. You tell Tim you would be happy to loan him $100, but it will cost him $5 in interest for you to carry his debt. Tim writes you an IOU slip for $105 and you give him a $100 bill. Later that day, you decide you want your money back faster than next week because you want to buy a new entertainment center. You ask around the break room to see if someone will buy Tim's $105 debt from you for $103. Someone jumps at the chance to make $2 for holding Tim's debt for a few more days. You didn't make the $5 interest you originally wanted, but you made $3 and you can go ahead and buy the entertainment center you've been eyeing. Selling Tim's IOU is exactly how the debt market works. Money continually flows through the system and spreads the risk of loaning money for mortgages out among several companies.

Not only was there plenty of credit available to buy houses before 2007, but there were also funds available to build houses. I had always thought that developing property would be something I would do someday in the far-off future. The risk with property development is, what if you buy a parcel of land, build something, and no one wants to buy it? Rental houses are much less risky. You buy a house in an existing neighborhood where people already live, so you know that people want to live in that neighborhood. What if I could do both things at once? What if I built new homes in the neighborhood around Carver House?

I could not build houses on top of existing homes, but there were still properties that needed to be developed—crack houses. I would buy up the neighborhood's crack houses, evict the tenants, and bulldoze the structures to the ground. After all the bad memories that happened on that property had been erased, I would build a new home. These structures would be affordable for those who lived in the community. Some people would refer to these as starter homes, but I have never liked that term. All some folks need is a two-bedroom with a bath and a half. There is nothing wrong with that.

No one should be shamed into thinking they were behind in life because they've lived twenty years in a "starter home."

I got excited about the prospects of repurposing the crack house properties. I wondered what getting rid of the crack houses would do for the community. I also looked at what the project could do for me personally. I had learned through my experience at Carver House that if you try to do too many things at once, something is bound to fall through the cracks. Maybe if I had not been trying to fit the Carver House renovations into my two fast-food job schedules, I would have seen Raj for who he was. I needed to make some changes if I was going to make the crack house deal work.

The Apostle John, while sitting on the island of Patmos, gave some practical life advice for being half in and half out of any situation:

> "So, because you are lukewarm—neither hot nor cold—I am about to spit you out of my mouth.—Revelations 3:16 (NIV)

The advice was given to those who are Sunday-morning type Christians whose faith does not follow their walk in life. I was doing something similar with my fast-food jobs and in real estate. I didn't want to be successful at fast food and own a franchise like my old boss, Mr. Daughtry. I kept working at McDonald's and Back Yard Burgers because I was addicted to the paychecks. I don't mean that my lifestyle had outstripped my means and I had to have the income from the two jobs to survive. I could live frugally on what I was making from the rental properties I owned. I was addicted to the illusion of security a steady paycheck provides.

I've often heard that the one thing that keeps someone from achieving their dreams is fear. Being afraid of failure, or success for that matter, is only one side of the coin. The other component of not taking a chance is giving up the security of a life you know. I would argue that someone's need for stability and predictability kills more dreams than fear does. I know it did for me. Even though the work at McDonald's and Back Yard Burgers was difficult and the hours long, the paychecks I received from those jobs were a safety net. If a tornado destroyed all of my properties tomorrow, I could still live comfortably with my fast-food jobs. Success is rarely achieved in comfortable surroundings, and I was determined to accomplish great things.

Burning My Boats

History tells us that 16th century Spanish explorer Hernán Cortés ordered his ship to be burned after landing on the shores of what is now Mexico. Cortés was afraid that his men might want to turn back and go home. If there were no boats to sail back home, Cortés's me had no other option than to go forward. Now, neither did I. I quit both McDonald's and Back Yard Burgers. The only income I had would be what I earned from real estate. I burned my own ships and the only direction I had was to go forward.

I revisited the playbook I had been using from the start. I contacted the bank officer I had worked with for the past few years about securing loans. While he had not been on board with the magnitude of the Carver House project, he was all about tearing down crack houses. I'm sure the bank was interested in improving the property values of a neighborhood they held a majority of the mortgages on. Should someone default on their mortgage, the bank would be able to sell the property for a higher value. Higher property values also meant that homeowners could get more credit on home equity lines of credit (HELOC). That means potentially hundreds of homeowners in the neighborhood could borrow money to fix up their houses.

I left the bank feeling confident in my decision to focus all of my attention on this project. For the next week, I called some of the contractors I had worked with on the Carver House project to get their recommendations for firms that specialized in residential demolition. I spoke with the local codes department to see what permits I would need to raze the crack house to the ground. The water, gas, and electric utilities would have to get involved in capping off services to the houses for safety reasons. It felt like there were a thousand details I needed to learn about or get set into motion before the project started.

Most importantly, I spent time in the neighborhoods talking to the residents and how the crack houses were impacting their lives. Everyone I spoke with was simply afraid. It's funny how the media portrays the dealers as being the intimidating element in the drug culture. They're no saints, but it's the addicts everyone was afraid of. It's the drug addicts that break into houses looking for something to sell and get their next fix. It's the addicts that skulk around ATMs waiting to rob someone who had just withdrawn some cash. And it was an addict that came up to my car one day while I was at turning in to get gas.

It was a nice day out, and I had my windows down. My mind was filled with facts and figures about the project, so I wasn't paying much attention to what was going on around me. There was a blur in my peripheral vision. I honestly thought it was a bug flying through my window, but it turned out the be the barrel of a gun. I don't remember what the person looked like or if he said anything. The barrel of the gun did all the talking for him. I knew if I either gave up my car or let this person in, there was a good likelihood I would end up dead.

My foot hit the gas pedal before I consciously decided to react. My car must have been as scared as I was, because I had no idea the little hoopty had that much pickup. I think I blew through a traffic light and stop sign before I calmed down enough to pull over. I might have cried or thrown up. I cannot remember. What I do recall is feeling mad. I was risking my future by taking a chance on this neighborhood. This—this is how they repaid me?

I tried to center myself and thought about what mattered. I gave a prayer of thanksgiving to the Lord. There is no way I could have made it out of that situation without God's help. Furthermore,

I realized that was exactly why I wanted to tear down the crack houses in the first place. What I had just experienced is what the residents of this neighborhood dealt with every day. Being a solid working-class citizen should not mean you're exposed to that level of risk driving to the corner store. Instead of scaring me off, the incident steeled my purpose. I doubled my efforts to move forward with the project.

As I moved though the process of securing financing and permits, I thought no one in the neighborhood noticed what I was doing. No matter what you do in life, for good or ill, people always take notice. I didn't realize that until I got a call from a reporter at the *Daily Herald*. Columbia's newspaper wanted to do a story on my revitalization efforts. I was finally getting the recognition that I should have gotten when Raj stole my thunder with the Carver House project.

The *Daily Herald's* article was like others pieces I'd seen before. The thinking-outside-the-box young entrepreneur tackleing a problem with a unique solution angle is the bread and butter of business journalism. I hoped the article would raise awareness of the drug problem in Columbia, but there was still something not settled in my soul.

It was that feeling you get when you drive away from your house and wonder if you left the oven on. I couldn't put my finger on what was causing the anxious flutters in my heart. I set my feelings aside and attributed it all to being nervous about burning my ships to go forward. That might have been the cause of my disquiet, but looking back, I believe it was a storm I always knew was coming.

The Financial Crisis of 2007–8

If you are going to be involved in real estate, or any other business venture, you have to keep up with and understand the news. Things that happen halfway around the world can affect your business as much as a town council zoning vote. Even fashion and social trends change the way we do business. Do you remember seeing any of the tall skinny homes being built ten years ago? An increase in population to the Middle Tennessee area and a housing shortage prompted a movement in architecture that changed how people live. To be successful in any business, you must foresee these trends and react to change. If you ignore or miss the shift in the wind, you are liable to be left behind.

I didn't fully appreciate how much world and national-level events mattered in the little town of Columbia, Tennessee until 2007. It's difficult to understand exactly what happened to cause the breakdown of banks "too big to fail" or the mighty General Motors being on the brink of collapse. The easy-to-understand answer is that everyone in the country was taking advantage of lower interest rates to build new homes. There were so many new homes on the market, there weren't enough buyers for all of them. When there are more sellers than buyers in any market, prices for what's being sold fall. This situation generally doesn't happen in the real estate market, or at least it does not happen on a national level. When the housing market started going soft, the Federal Reserve raised interest rates to compensate for riskier home loans. As money got more expensive to borrow, home loans became harder to come by.

What killed the economy in 2007–8 wasn't just because money was more expensive to borrow. When interest rates were low, banks issued variable interest rate mortgages to customers that had a greater risk of defaulting on their loans. The monthly payment on variable rate mortgages changes with the interest rate the Federal Reserve charges banks to borrow money. When interest rates started going up, people who had variable-rate mortgages saw their monthly payments increase. Many of those people couldn't afford the extra payments and folks started defaulting on their mortgages. The system of Fannie Mae and Freddie Mac selling off mortgage debt started to grind to a halt. Because of the mounting mortgage defaults, no one wanted to buy mortgage debt. Suddenly, no one wanted to lend money to anyone for any reason.

Almost every company that exists in a capitalistic economy requires debt to function. Imagine you are running a company that produces flowerpots. You have a $10,000 order for a shipment of pots that will be paid in a month. It costs you $4,000 to produce those pots, but you do not have the funds to complete the order. You contact your bank, and they will loan you the $4,000 for a month and charge you $100 interest. That is not a bad deal considering you are more than doubling your money on this order. This is how many businesses operate, and operations cannot happen when there is no short-term money to borrow.

When there was no money to lend because of the increased defaults on mortgages, the entire economy of the United States suffered. Companies that couldn't survive without taking out short-term debt had to either scale back their operations or shut down completely. This meant that more people couldn't make their mortgage payments because their hours were cut or they lost their jobs completely. The country ran the risk of entering a total meltdown that would have made the Great Depression in the 1920s and '30s look like a bad day at the office.

All the economic gloom and doom seemingly happened overnight. It felt like one day it was business as usual and the next day, everything had changed. There were signs that the economy was about to tank, but I did not notice them. Even if I had taken notice, it might not have mattered to me. I had secured my financing from my local bank for tearing down the crack houses. I had enough money to complete that project. If I had to sit on the houses a couple of years before they sold, that would be fine. I could either rent them out or simply rely on the income from my other rental properties. I would be fine.

I held to that illusion until I got the word the bank officer whom I had been dealing with all these years had committed suicide. It is horribly sad that anyone would feel taking their own life was a viable solution to any problem. I prayed for his family and continued with my project. A week or two before I was to tear down the first crack house, I was asked to a meeting at my bank. This was not unusual. With a high-profile project that the bank is publicly linked to, I would commonly go in and give everyone a status update.

I could tell that something had changed when I got to the bank. Being a local institution, everyone pretty much knew everyone else. I had done enough business there that I'd be greeted by a couple of employees when I ended. Today, there was no reception. The bank's lobby always had some lame instrumental music playing, but there was nothing playing today. I was about to walk up to one of the tellers and say something when one of the bank's officers greeted me. He directed me to his office, where we were to talk.

I didn't have much of a chance to say anything once we were seated. The bank officer started off with, "James, there's no easy way to tell you this. . ."

The conversation was one-sided, and it felt like I'd been taken to the principal's office. The bank officer was incredibly apologetic but told me the bank did a complete audit of my prior loan officer's accounts after his death. It seemed that he was playing fast and loose with loan paperwork. I never found out if there were any true improprieties, such as embezzlement, going on. I was told that there were serious inconsistencies in my prior loan officer's work. I'm sure the beginning of the Financial Crisis caused the bank to examine their newer loans. These were the loans they not been able to sell to Fannie Mae and Freddie Mac. The bank was on the hook for all their new loans and would have to collect directly from the debtors. Reevaluation of loans under all these circumstances was a wise move. Unfortunately, I was caught in a hailstorm of bad circumstances.

Since the housing market was in the toilet, my original loan officer should never have issued me the loans in the first place. The loan officer I was currently speaking with told me the bank was calling in the loan. Legally, banks or other lending institutions can demand payment of a loan in full at any time if that is part of the loan agreement. Calling a loan due is usually not done unless there has been a violation of the loan agreement. If a bank got a reputation for calling loans whenever they felt like it, soon no one would come to them to borrow money.

The Other Shoe Drops

The 2007–8 Financial Crisis, coupled with whatever impropriety my previous loan office had been involved with, was sufficient reason for my bank to call in the crack house loans. I believe I was offered the option to offer a hefty cash surety to keep the loans active. This would mean that I would have to secure the present loans with a pile of money I didn't have. The bank officer did give me the opportunity to find a buyer for the houses. I would have a few weeks to find buyers, and if I could not sell, the bank would foreclose. I realized the bank could be the proud owners of a group of crack houses in the Carver House neighborhood. I wonder what the *Daily Herald* would think of that.

I put those mean-spirited thoughts out of my head as I left the bank. I was reacting to being betrayed once again. The conversation I had with the bank officer was worse than my final conversation with Raj. With Raj, I had been betrayed by a person. We all fall short of living an ethical life or making good decisions from time to time. Even though I hated Raj duping me, I could forgive him because he's as much as flawed human as anyone else. My faith is based on the concept that we all sin and fall short of the glory of God, but we can be forgiven through His love. Yes, forgiving and understanding Raj's shortcomings was one thing.

Feeling betrayed by an institution is a different kind of hurt. It felt like the Postal Service had turned a blind eye toward a mail carrier they knew was snooping through someone else's mail. You're not only betrayed by the person looking through your mail. Everyone at the Post Office who allowed it to go on has betrayed you too. That is how I felt with the bank. We entrust our money is kept safe when we deposit it in a bank. We expect that everyone at a bank is working for our best interests and want us to succeed. I have no evidence that anyone else at the bank knew my original loan officer was letting things slide. As often happens in businesses, if you are hitting or exceeding your performance goals, you get congratulations and little scrutiny.

I couldn't let being bitter over circumstances cloud my judgment. I had to act as if I was going to get myself out of this mess. I started making phone calls. I called everyone I could think of that might to buy the crack houses. I even made calls to people who might know someone who wanted to get into the real estate business. I checked with local realtors who might have a line on a buyer. No one on my list was interested in buying the properties, but I did have a few folks that promised to pass along the news to others that might be interested. All I could do now was wait—precious days passed without hearing from anyone. I found out that I was not good at waiting. There was always some play to make, angle to work, or plain old hard work to get me out of most situations. There was nothing to do except watch the clock and hope for the best.

I did receive a phone call. One of my contacts had gotten through to a small holding company that was interested in hearing my pitch. I set up a meeting and presented the same research I had initially given the bank. The numbers were solid and even with the soft housing market, there was no way they could lose the deal. We discussed signing paperwork for the sale in a few days. I couldn't have been happier. I would end up with a few dollars profit from the sale, but most importantly, the bank would not have to foreclose. That night I slept well for the first time in weeks.

I slept late the next morning. The stress of the last few weeks had left me exhausted, and I sorely needed a reset. I laid in bed for a few minutes and started daydreaming about what would happen after the sale of the crack houses. On my nightstand, my phone started to vibrate. I figured whoever it was could wait a few minutes until I was awake, but the phone didn't stop vibrating. I shook my head and rubbed my eyes trying to focus on the small flip phone's screen. I had missed several calls and have a few voicemails. After I heard the messages, all I wanted to do was to go back to bed.

Overnight, there had been a shooting at one of the crack houses. Various friends and family had left messages about the news. No one knew if the shooting victim would live or die. One voicemail rolled into another until I heard the one I was waiting for. The holding company was pulling out of our deal. They knew the neighborhood was a little rough, but they didn't know how dangerous it was. So that was that. There were no offers for the properties. I made a call to the bank to set up a meeting about the terms of the foreclosure. I was only certain of one thing. I had burned my ships and I was out of options. I had no idea of what to do next.

Chapter Five
Subway

Bad news travels fast in a small town. It was not long before everyone knew the crack houses would not be torn down any time soon. The members of the neighborhood were sorely disappointed at the news. I felt like I had let everyone down who had bought into my dreams. I was able to come back from the Carver House incident fighting because I had never suffered a catastrophic setback. It's easier to get back on your feet and fight back if you've only known one defeat. You tell yourself that it was a one-time thing never to be repeated and you keep moving forward.

When a major setback hits you a second time, you begin to doubt your decision-making abilities and purpose. I began to overanalyze what had gotten me to this point. What didn't I do this? I should have seen that. Why did I quit both of my fast-food jobs? These were the questions that plagued the time before I went to sleep every night. I spent that time dreaming of what my future was going to look like.

The lack of a project and steady work only increased this anxiety. My entire adult life, I had worked eighty hours a week at the fast-food jobs plus dealing with my real estate holds. I suddenly did not know what to do with myself. There was not much to managing the properties I still owned. Those rental houses were in good condition. I periodically looked in on the properties and my tenants, but that was just busy work. I wanted to shut down for a while and take things easy. I deserved that—didn't I? It doesn't matter what we deserve or not, at times. The world marches on and circumstances change with no regard to what we want.

I mentioned earlier how interconnected the fates of General Motors' (GM) plant in Spring Hill were to Maury County. With the economy growing worse, I expected there to be a slow down at the factory. Times would be tight for most everyone associated with GM, but how could a crisis in the mortgage market affect one of the world's largest automakers? A large part of GM's business has nothing to do with the automotive industry. In 1919, GM formed the General Motors Acceptance Corporation (GMAC). This company existed to issue loans for GM cars. As GM's market share grew during the 20th century, GMAC's services also expanded. The finance arm of GM branched out into insurance, commercial finance, and home mortgages. GM and GMAC were tied together tightly enough that GMAC went belly up, so did GM.

General Motors scaled back its operations during the crisis and that sent ripples through the communities of Spring Hill and Columbia. Most of my tenants worked for or had jobs that depended on GM's operation. One by one, my tenant moved out of my rental properties. I could have stayed afloat if one of my properties was vacant, but I could not withstand a sudden exodus of the majority of my tenants. There was no other big industry that was thriving in Maury County, so there was no demand for my rental homes.

In times of crisis or natural disasters, there are always financial scavengers who have money to buy cheap, weather the current situation, and sell for large profits once things have gone back to normal. One of these carpetbaggers found out about my situation. I was forced to liquidate all my real estate holdings to keep the bank from foreclosing. I now knew how Job must have felt when everything was taken away from him. On the upside, I didn't have boils like Job did.

I did my best to turn to the Lord and ask for guidance. I did not understand why this was happening to me. I could have lived a quiet normal life working fast food, and this would not have happened to me. Should I have even tried to follow my dreams if all I was destined for was failure? I knew the answer to hard times was to have faith. We, like Job, cannot see God's complete plan for us. I had to have faith that He had better things in store for me.

I tried to remind myself that God worked through the strangest of vessels when my phone rang a few weeks after the loans were called. I'm surprised that I hadn't taken his number out of my phone, but Raj was calling me. I had no clue why he would be calling me other than to possibly gloat about liquidating my properties. I answered to a contrite and pleasant-sounding Raj. He told me that he had heard about my troubles and had an opportunity for me. Raj knew about my fast food experience and had a contact that was a bigwig at Subway. The chain was feeling the pinch of the Financial Crisis, like the rest of the country, and was reducing the initial franchisee investment amount. Raj went on to tell me that he had nothing to do with this opportunity but wanted to pass the information along to me.

I was not sure what to say to Raj. I wanted to believe that he felt bad for cheating me out of a fair share in the Carver House sale and wanted to make up for it. If Raj truly was not involved in the operation, his only interest might be a finder's fee from Subway. Clearing his conscience while making a buck was definitely something Raj would do. So, I took his friend's number and set up a meeting to talk Subway.

The meeting was all business. My Subway contact went over all the projected costs and revenue a Subway store was likely to make. Those figures were in normal financial times, but they still looked viable given the current economic situation. As the meeting went on, we discussed more of the day-to-day operations, approved vendors, and other managerial concerns. There was nothing that was outside my experience in food service, and I felt confident that I could make a go of it. At the end of the conversation, the Subway man told me that this was a special opportunity because he would have direct oversight of the franchise agreement. I had the feeling whatever his deal was, it might have followed the letter of Subway's franchise policies, but not necessarily the spirit of those codes.

I could live with someone moving a few corporate lines to help me set up a franchise. I was sure that opening up a new store in this economy would be a feather in the Subway man's cap—no matter how it was accomplished. Opening one more new store might also hit a bonus goal for this man. I felt this might be God's opportunity for me to have better days. I took all of the literature the Subway man provided and told him I would have an answer for him in a week or so. Before we parted, I asked if I could have a partner in the franchise. He said he did not see why I could not be a co-franchisee with someone else, and we went our separate ways.

After I left the meeting, I thought about everything that happened to me since high school. I wondered if everything had led me to this deal. Maybe my real estate dreams were a vehicle for the Lord to send me this opportunity. I thought about how ironic it was that I did not want to be a fast-food franchise owner like my old boss Mr. Daughtry. Perhaps I was being taught a lesson about humility with this opportunity. I was getting off track believing that I deserved a break after all of the hard work I'd put in. Maybe the Lord was reminding me what used to matter to me was the right path. I would pray on the matter and let the Lord guide my decision.

Subway

I spoke with my friend Terry about going in with me on the Subway franchise. One of the locations that was presented to me was on a highway not far from Columbia. The town had a manufacturing plant and cross traffic to support its operations. As we dug into the paperwork, we realized that we did not have enough money to cover the franchise fees. The answer was hidden in plain sight. I would move on and figure out some other way to get everything back I had lost.

I made a call to Raj and let him know that I could not afford the franchise. It was only right that I give him a heads up before letting his friend know the bad news. Raj sounded disappointed that I would not be taking the offer. I explained my financial situation, and Raj suddenly got excited. He told me that if it were a matter of money, he would stake me the franchise fees. The old saying "fool me once, shame on you; fool me twice, shame on me" kept running through my head as Raj made his pitch. I considered all of the angles Raj could be playing by loaning me the money. The only thing I could come up with was that if I defaulted on the loan, Raj would own half a Subway franchise. The only other thing I owned he could take away from me was a 2000 Honda Accord. Somehow, I didn't think that was his endgame. I genuinely believe Raj was trying to make up for the past. I quite literally had nothing to lose, so I agreed.

My friend Terry and I were the first Black franchise owners of a Subway in the state of Tennessee. I doubt that anyone else celebrated that milestone but for our families and us, but I was proud of the accomplishment. Moreover, I was thankful the Lord saw me through this crisis and taught me a lesson in the process. If someone who has wronged you reaches out to you, you should listen to what they have to say. That person may be asking for forgiveness or offer to make amends. We might be missing an opportunity for healing wounds if we do not take the time to listen. Certainly, my life was changed by putting aside any animosity I felt toward Raj and listening to him.

Terry and I started setting up the restaurant a few weeks later. Nothing could be left up to chance in the restaurant's setup. We had budgeted out the set up to nearly the penny, and we didn't have any backup capital. Plumbers, electricians, and general contractors paraded in and out of the space for a few weeks. My experience with the Carver House renovations and with McDonald's gave me an advantage in overseeing all aspects of the restaurant's setup. I knew that everything had to be perfect for the health inspectors to certify we were compliant to open. Something seemingly trivial like having a cracked tile around a sink, or a faucet taking a couple of seconds too long to supply hot water, would be grounds to deny us a food service permit.

We also had to worry about ringing all the bells of our Subway franchise agreement. Subway, like any company that offers franchises, wants customers to have a consistent experience at all of their restaurants. There will be some regional differences in menus and local weekly specials in any restaurant chain. But a customer should expect the same quality of food and service if they walk into a Subway in New York or Tennessee. That means that all of a chain's restaurants have to have standardized décor, food suppliers, employee training, and customer flow through the restaurant. There are hundreds of items on franchise checklists that owners are graded on by corporate office inspectors. Many franchise agreements state that too many violations of these items for a long enough period of time can cause a franchisee to lose ownership of the restaurant.

If preparing the restaurant for the opening was not stressful enough, my personal funds were rapidly depleting. I budgeted that my savings would hold out until a few days before the restaurant's opening. That was if everything went well and there were no unexpected expenses. Terry had sunk everything he had into the restaurant too, so we were broke together. There wasn't a single penny we found on the sidewalk that didn't end up in our pockets. I set up situations where I would be at someone's house around dinner time hoping they would offer me a meal. For weeks I didn't spend a dime on a stick of gum or anything that wasn't a necessity. I still don't know how Terry and I survived those days.

Within a few weeks, all of the work was completed and we passed inspections from the health department and Subway. We could not afford to do a soft open or a fancy grand opening. There would not be a ribbon-cutting ceremony or pony rides in the parking lot. There was no other alternative but to open the restaurant and start making sandwiches as soon as we could get a food truck in. To advertise the grand opening, we just talked to people.

There are few stereotypes that hold true about small-town America. The one that does hold water is that people living in small towns are incredibly sensitive to change. When we were starting to build out the restaurant's dining room, a few of the town's residents would stick their heads in the front door and ask what we were doing. This wasn't done maliciously. Folks that live in a small town are sensitive to change and information was all they were looking for. Everyone we spoke with was excited about Subway coming in. Pretty soon, we had other residents of the town driving by to check out our progress. That's all I needed to prove small towns have a fast-moving internal communications system. To announce the grand opening, we tapped into the same network and let them do our advertising for us.

A few days before the grand opening, Terry and I were putting our first full Subway food order together. We had to order everything from either Subway or a local vendor Subway had approved. The order restrictions were partially to ensure all Subways are using quality produces. The other reason deals with how large businesses make money. Subway, and any large company, cuts costs is by what businesspeople call economies of scale. The theory is that if I go to the grocery store to buy a tomato, I'll pay a dollar a pound. If Subway approaches a corporate farm and wants to buy a ton of tomatoes, the farm might sell that quantity for forty cents a pound. Selling to one customer is less risky than trying to sell smaller quantities to multiple customers. It's a good deal for the farmer and for Subway. Subway uses the buying power of thousands of stores and gets to spread cheaper food costs out through all their restaurants. The cheaper it costs to make a sandwich, the more profit Subway makes.

I knew about the supply chain before getting into the franchise agreement. What I missed was that food orders were cash on delivery (COD). We could either prepay the order with a credit card or give the driver a cashier's check or money order. The first order was close to $1,500, and we had three days to come up with the money. The problem was that Terry and I were broke. We were so broke that I figured I had exactly enough gas to make it from now to the grand opening. If we did not make any money when we opened our doors, I would be walking home that night.

The First Bet

Without a dime between us, I had no clue where I would come up with the $1,500 for the food order. I couldn't ask Raj, my family, or anyone I knew for that kind of money. I had used up about every favor I had. There was one angle I had left to play. Growing up where I did, I met all sorts of folks whose professions were on the underside of legality. Maybe I could borrow money from one of those people. I knew the interest rate would be high, but we'd make it back within a few days of the grand opening. I floated the idea past Terry and he came up with an idea that sounded less risky at the time. I could borrow $500 and place a bet on the NBA playoff game that night. The Milwaukee Bucks were playing the Atlanta Hawks. The Hawks were the underdogs. If the Hawks won, I'd make back enough money to pay the loan and cover the food truck. If the Hawks lost, I was out $500 instead of the full $1,500.

Terry was talking in desperation logic, but somehow it made sense. I probably could not get anyone to loan me the full $1,500 anyway. I made a few calls, and by noon everything was set. I drove home that night feeling like I had swallowed an entire bag of marshmallows. What had I done? What was I going to do if the Hawks lost? I prayed that everything would work out.

I almost could not watch the game that night. It sounds silly, but I felt like watching would somehow change the outcome of the game. I did not know if watching would be to the Hawk's detriment or benefit. Watching could not hurt anything, could it? I decided to chance it and turned on the television. I have been watching sports my entire life, but I'd never experienced anything like I during that playoff game. I was invested in the outcome of every play. When the Bucks scored, it was like someone shoved a hot needle in my gut. If the Hawks caught a penalty, I was outraged beyond reason.

When the Hawks scored or something went their way, it was like taking the first bite of a good steak.

For over two hours, I sat watching the Bucks and Hawks battle it out. Never before had I had that wide range of emotions tightly packed into that short a time period. When the Hawks won, I thought I would lose my mind. The excitement and relief I felt almost made me want to cry. I made a little north of $2,000 on that $500 bet. Above and beyond the obvious ability to pay back the loan and get the restaurant's food truck, I was a winner again. I felt like I was in control of my life for the first time in months.

I paid for the food truck, and the grand opening went as smoothly as possible. The first time you go live with any food service venture, there are bound to be problems. One of the biggest was that I had less than $10 in change for the register. That was all the money I had left over from the gambling winnings. Terry and I handled the change issue and other problems out as the day went on. Even though we were frantically trying to learn our job duties with real customers, everything seemed to fit. I got in the groove of helping customers and chatting everyone up. All our customers that day thanked us for being there. Big-city chains in small towns make the residents feel a little more connected with the outside world, and they appreciated our service to the community.

We didn't do as much business that day as I had anticipated, but with the reaction we received, I knew we'd be successful. There was enough money in the till that Terry and I issued ourselves petty cash vouchers for gas. I had been right. Neither of us would have made it home that night with the gas we had in our tanks. The gas money was literally all the money I had in the world. It kept me in the game for another day and for that, I was thankful.

Chapter Six
The Hustle

It took Terry and me a couple of weeks to feel like we were in control of the Subway business. Lunchtime, of course, was when we were the busiest. We noticed that we weren't getting as much lunch traffic from the local factory as we would have expected. I asked one of the factory workers who did come in for lunch why I didn't see more of his friends in. He told me that their lunch breaks weren't long enough to drive over, wait in line, eat lunch, and get back in time to clock back in. That meant that none of the local restaurants were capitalizing on the factory's lunch business. If the factory workers couldn't come to us, we would go to them.

As soon as we got a couple of people hired to handle our in-house lunch business, Terry and I would get to the store earlier than usual. We did our prep work for the day and then started to make sandwiches. We made plain lettuce, tomato, a meat, and American cheese sandwiches on white bread. We put those in boxes with a bag of chips and a cookie. Every day at lunch, we'd sit in a vacant lot next to the factory selling those lunch boxes for $5. We'd carry a cooler full of bottled sodas out with us as an add-on sale. The factory workers loved it. It wasn't anything fancy, but it was an economical lunch solution to people on a time crunch.

We were successful enough at the boxed lunches, we expanded our catering options. Dinner time was fairly dead around the restaurant, so we got in contact with every local venue we could think of that had a nighttime event. If the middle school had a play, we'd offer to do a sandwich tray for the cast party. When the town council had meetings, we called around to take their dinner orders. Funeral homes, Masonic lodges, birthday parties, churches, and wherever more than five people gathered together, we offered free delivery catering. Before too long, our nighttime business was as busy as our lunch rushes.

Before too long, our little, small town Subway franchise was turning a profit. I was able to repay Raj's seed money in no time. Terry and I didn't have to worry about gas money or where our next meal was coming from. I was taking in enough money that I made a few more bets on games. The dollar amounts were nothing huge like my first bet. Gambling on games was a fun little hobby. Putting a wager on any sporting event automatically raised the intensity level of watching the game. It was my version of having a beer or two with the game on. I found out that I had a talent for picking winners. I was making more than I lost, so it was like a hobby that was paying dividends.

The Big Time

After a while, the Subway franchise became profitable enough that Terry and I could afford to hire enough staff to cover store operations. Neither of us had to work from long before open to way past closing time anymore. We were doing so well we were getting bonuses from Subway for hitting all of our numbers. I had money again and felt good about myself. All of the hard work and turmoil I'd had over the last few years should be rewarded. This was no go-out-and-try-sushi type rewards like I had done before. I wanted to travel and experience what the world had to offer.

My first big trip was to New York City. The movies and TV shows don't do the town justice. For the first time in my life, I felt physically small walking down the streets of Manhattan. The press of people and the height of the buildings make you initially feel insignificant. Once you push past the emotions of feeling like you cannot possibly matter in a city this size, you begin to feel like anything is possible. The art, architecture, and action of the city remind you that humans created all of this. From *The Lion King* musical I saw to the Empire State Building, man created these things. I was energized. I wanted more out of life than a single Subway franchise.

When I got back home, I started to look for other Subway franchising opportunities. If I had turned a single Subway into an unexpected success, I could do it for another one. Terry wasn't interested in being responsible for a second location, so my connections at Subway hooked me up with another person that wanted to go half in on a franchise. This time around I knew exactly how

I wanted everything set up and how the store needed to be run. I tapped into the same practices I had developed in our first store to make the second one an immediate success.

Detroit

I looked in on both operations from time to time, but the staff we hired was self-sufficient. Things were running smoothly enough that neither store needed my help other than the occasional question or catastrophe that needed solving. I found myself betting more frequently and with bigger amounts. I was not placing bets with some back-alley bookie. I was making legal bets on internet sites overseas. Technically speaking, I was placing the bet in the Cayman Islands, Luxembourg, or wherever it was legal to gamble. I would wire money to an overseas account, and my winnings were deposited back here in the United States. I paid taxes on my winnings and legally could deduct gambling losses from my income tax.

I thought I was living a good life. I did not know it then, but I was bored. I had everything I could possibly want in life, but I still felt an emptiness inside that needed to be filled. I had run out of things to conquer, so I invented something. By this time, the country was past the Finical Crisis of 2007–8. The government bailouts had happened for the big companies, but many communities had yet to recover. Detroit was one of these cities. GM was still reeling from filing bankruptcy, and the American automotive industry was in shambles. Many automaker jobs had gone overseas or to Mexico and a significant portion of Detroit's residence up and moved away. To give you an idea, in 1950, Detroit's population was 1.9 million. In 2013, the city of Detroit had slightly fewer than 800,000 residents. This left over 78,000 vacant houses in the city. There were entire neighborhoods in Detroit that were only home to stray dogs and cats.

Nationwide, the housing market was barely getting back on its feet. It was a good time to buy a home if you had the money to do so. With the glut of houses in the ghost town of Detroit, you could buy a house for $1. A solitary dollar would get you a quitclaim deed for a house in your hand within twenty-four hours. How could I not make money in an environment like this? I called up Terry and told him to back his bags for Detroit.

The flight to Detroit was less than two hours. When we touched down at Detroit's Wayne County airport, I was anxious to see the city. We rented a car at the airport, and I thought it was telling that we were given a Toyota. Terry and I wanted to drive around the city to get a feel for what we were getting ourselves into. As inspiring as New York had been for me, Detroit felt soul-crushing. The city that had contributed to making America a world leader in manufacturing was like a sick grandmother. Long past her prime, the grandmother's children had moved away and there was no one left to look after her.

Terry and I checked into a hotel across the street from a casino. We might need a distraction in the evening, and casinos always had shows and cheap buffets. I'd told Terry that my plan was to go out and look at properties during the day and research Detroit's multiple listing service (MLS) by night. A region's MLS is a directory of properties for sale. It is like the old magazines that you could list a car for sale but for real estate. Detroit's MLS was almost like a phone book, and I had no idea where any of these properties were in relationship to each other.

The next morning, I would get a city map at the gas station. For tonight I felt we needed to ease into our Detroit experience. I suggested to

Terry we catch a cheap dinner at the casino and hit work hard tomorrow morning. Terry agreed, and we walked across the street. When you first enter a casino, there is an unmistakable hum. The noise isn't only from current passing through neon lights. The purr is of human energy. The click of craps dice shaking in someone's hand to the scrape of a blackjack hand comes through once you open a casino's doors. I know I had imagined that, but that's how my brain was interpreting what I was feeling.

Terry and I did hit the casino's cheap buffet and did not return back to our rooms until early the next morning. I could not help myself. The casino was like Disneyland to me. I did not have to wait on the outcome of a game and a wire transfer to get my winnings. It all happened in real-time, and that night I was on a streak. Terry and I both quit while we were ahead that night. It felt like it was an omen of things to come in the Motor City.

Motor City Blues

When we finally woke up the next day, I went out to review properties that looked promising. I was disappointed in the condition of everything I saw. One house had all of the copper pipes and electrical wire stripped from it. In another house, the appliances you would expect to stay with a house when a tenant moved out—dishwashers, water heaters, and the like—had disappeared too. It was evident that a couple of the houses had squatters. The good news was most of the homes I saw were still structurally sound. Refurbishing a house with good bones is doable. Trying to raise a house from the dead was not something I had the time or inclination to do.

I'd make some decisions on properties tomorrow. The sun was starting to set, and I didn't want to be caught in no man's land after dark. I got back to the hotel, and Terry and I hit the casino again. One of the pit bosses recognized us from the night before and gave us a discount on a room at the casino. Why not? A discount was a discount, and we were there to make money. We accepted and moved in the next day. We would live at the casino for the next two months.

The two months that followed were much like our first and second days in Detroit. I would get up at some point during the day, go out and look at properties, then we would hit the casino until early the following morning. If we ran low on money, one of us would call the Subway and get someone to wire us money. If I needed something, I'd walk into the casino store and buy something. The store staff would snap to like I was royalty whenever I walked in. It was like I was Richard Gere in *Pretty Woman*. Everyone in the casino catered to my every need.

Every day I intended to buy a house or two to fix up, but something always kept me from doing it. One day I was touring properties and stopped at one house as it started to rain. I tried the front door, and luckily it was not locked. I walked in just as the light rain turned into a downpour. Wandering around, I heard the unmistakable sound of water dripping in the living room. I went in to see how bad the leak was. The sound of water turned from a drip to a waterfall. It was dark inside the house, so I took a flashlight out I always carried with me to see what was going on. Flowing down the walls of the living room was a red liquid. It was like someone on the second floor was pouring a bucket down the wall—that's how fast it was coming down. I was, and still am, 99 percent sure the liquid was blood. It was like I had stepped into a Stephen King book. I almost slipped on wet carpet trying to get out of the house.

After that, I did not go out looking at properties for a few days. I had a different tact in mind. I would just buy a couple of houses for the listing. Everything I was seeing was cheap enough it didn't matter if one of the houses was a dog. I called the realtor and set up a meeting. By lunchtime the next day, I had bought my first property since the crack houses back in Columbia.

I called a contractor who the realtor recommended and met him at my new purchases the next day. I had not done so bad buying blind. The contractor and I set a plan of action for the house and went out to buy supplies. We locked them up in the house, and the contractor made plans to start on the renovations the next day. I was back in real estate, and it felt like old times. I'd put a few thousand in these houses, sell them to someone cheap, and still make money on the deal. I hit the casino that night but didn't stay out too late. I had a big day tomorrow.

Except I did not have a big day. All the building materials we had bought the day before were stolen overnight. Less than half of the contractor's crew showed up for work that day too. I have a feeling the absent half of the crew was out selling my materials or using them on another job. Theft, or some other impediment, would happen with every property I invested in over the next few weeks. Squatters wouldn't move out of one house. The knot of leins on some properties made them impossible to work on.

Possibly the biggest roadblock to purchasing cheap real estate in Detroit was the property taxes. Even though houses were being sold in Detroit for less than a movie ticket, that didn't mean the county's tax assessed value of the house wasn't at normal market prices. That meant that the property tax bills on some of these houses were in the thousands. I could not afford to sit on real estate that I couldn't develop and pay the tax bills.

The nights of gambling were not going well either. I was losing more than I was gaining there too. Every time we called back to Tennessee to have the Subway wire us more money, the management sounded increasingly hesitant. We had taken enough away from the business the stores were having problems paying their bills. After two months of living in a casino and trying to single-handedly reinvigorate Detroit's real estate market, we had to go home.

When I arrived back in Tennessee, I had exactly $180 in my pocket. That was all the money I had in the world. Needless to say, my behavior in Detroit cost me my interests in both Subway franchises. I was worse off now than I was after the crack house deal went bad. Financially my situation was more dire than ever, and I had an added problem—I had a jonesing to place one more bet.

Chapter Seven
The Long Road Home

I had to start over.

When I say start over, I mean that I had less money in my pocket and future prospects than when I left high school. I could not afford a place of my own, so I moved back in with family. I had no income, so I did the only thing I knew I could fall back on. I was welcomed back, but not fully with open arms. My family was full of questions about my financial demise. The answers I gave were truthful, but vague. When you have any addiction problem, you learn how to tell just enough of the truth to stop any further questions.

Starting over included applying at McDonald's and Back Yard Burgers. I was welcomed back to both restaurant chains, but I had lost ground there too. When I left both jobs, I was a supervisor. Coming back, I was a new hire who had a few skills. Whenever someone puked in the bathroom, I got to clean it up. Every day I worked, I was embarrassed that my life had come back around to this. I should have been thankful that I had the means to support myself. Instead, I was bitter that I had lost everything. I thought I could get everything back the same way I had lost it. I kept gambling.

You might have thought that I had hit rock bottom when I returned from Detroit. I had not. Rock bottom does not happen when you believe that your addiction is the way out of your present situation. I held to the belief that gambling would accelerate my getting back into the real estate business. I saw my losses and gains from gambling as I would any ordinary business expense or revenue. Isn't gambling the same as starting a business, purchasing stock, or investing in real estate? I told myself that since all these activities are risky, there is no ethical difference between them. I wish now I had understood how wrong I was.

The Rules of Gambling

When you invest in a stock, real estate, or start a business, there is risk. You are buying something tangible when you make these investments. If you purchase a stock, you are buying fractional ownership in that company. Let us say there were 100 shares of XYZ Limited for sale and you purchased five shares. You now own 5 percent of XYZ's assets, liabilities, and profits. As an owner, you have certain rights to the net proceeds of the company should it go out of business. You also are providing funds to XYZ to grow their operations through a stock purchase. You are giving XYZ Limited the opportunity to hire more employees and fuel other businesses through purchasing equipment or raw materials. These are all good and ethical outcomes of investing in XYZ Limited.

When you place a bet, you are purchasing a chance at a future profit. Once the sporting event is over, dice are thrown, or cards are put on the table, there is no value to your bet. The money you bet goes on to further expand a legal, or illegal, gambling enterprise. The proceeds from illegal gambling are likely to fund other illegal activities such as prostitution, loan sharking, or drugs. Legal gambling operations don't exist to provide you a platform to get rich. Casinos and sportsbooks are businesses that profit from their customers' losses.

There is another key difference between gambling and investing in a legitimate business venture—intent. Someone with an addictive personality does not gamble to make money. That person gambles to meet psychological needs. For me, gambling was like the morning's first cup of coffee. Looking through the listings was like smelling the fresh coffee brewing. Some mornings you can almost feel the caffeine kick in after that first sip. That was the rush I felt when placing a bet. Finishing your first cup was like watching the game. Just like drinking your morning coffee, gambling was a ritual for me.

If you are a coffee drinker, imagine what mornings without that first cup are like. Aside from the caffeine rush, if you do not have that morning ritual, nothing feels like it is going to go well that day. There is nothing magic about having a cup of coffee that makes your day go well. But you'll blame everything from catching red lights to forgetting your lunch on missing your coffee. Gamblers hold to similar superstitions. Wearing your lucky shirt on game day, flipping a light switch on and off seven times, or doing any other compulsive act to bring you luck is within most gamblers' minds. These habitual behaviors cause their own problems when the ritual fails to give you the luck you think you deserve. You feel like you have failed yourself by not performing the lucky behavior correctly. If your lucky behavior was flicking the light switch seven times and lost your bet, you must have flicked the light switch six times.

All those feelings are outside of winning or losing your bet. Winning brings validation to the enterprise of gambling. How could you not feel like you are justified in placing a bet when a $20 "investment" returned $100? The winning feelings never seem to cover all the times you lose. Do you remember being called to the chalkboard to work on a math problem during elementary school? Losing a bet is like getting that math problem wrong. The entire class is looking at you. The kids start to giggle because you could not get the problem right. That's what it feels like when you lose a bet. Not only are you embarrassed that you made a bad bet, but there is also the shame of continuing to bet.

Somewhere inside my mind, there was a rational voice that told me gambling was wrong and I should stop. There comes the point on the downslope of an addiction you are tired of the behavior. Every bet is going to be your last because you just need the money for one more. . . There is always a "one more" justification in gambling. You need the money for one more rent or car payment. It did not matter what the "one more" was. You always kept gambling for another "one more" that came down the pike.

Getting to Rock Bottom

My biggest "one more" was thinking I was one more bet from getting everything back. That is a dangerous position to be in because there was a purpose behind my gambling. I tried to hide my activities from the family that was housing me, but there were times I could not. When you're working eighty hours a week and keep coming up broke, they knew what time it was. Still, I kept gambling because that's what addicts do.

The trick to being an addict is trying to make your life look normal while maintaining your addiction. I went to church when my work schedule would allow. There were family functions and dinners I attended. I tried not to place bets on sporting events that happened when I knew I had an event to attend. I did not want to be tempted to look at the scores of games I'd bet on. I even tried dating a little more during this time. I thought a good woman's love might help me kick the habit.

As chance would have it, I did meet someone at a Subway. I was grabbing a quick dinner at one of the Subways in Columbia. I was walking out the door when I saw a gorgeous woman walking in. She was pretty enough that it felt like a baseball bat had hit me in the chest when I saw her. As she got closer to the door, I not so smoothly held the door open for her and asked for her number. She politely declined giving me her phone number. I was devastated that I'd missed my chance with this young lady. I do not know if she sensed my disappointment or was interested in me, but she told me that if I wanted to see her again, I could visit her church on Sunday. The next Sunday, I made it to her church's Sunday service.

A few years later, we would be married in the same church we had our first "date." When I stood at the altar with her, I couldn't believe she would marry me. She wasn't like the women I had known before. She was interested in who I was and not what was in my bank account. She knew about my past real estate glories and wanted me to get back there again. That wasn't because of the extra income real estate could give us. She wanted to be a partner in achieving our dreams together. That's the sort of person you want to spend the rest of your life with.

We did forge a life together even though I was still gambling. The strange thing is I thought her love would make me want to quit. Don't get me wrong, I did want to stop. There were now a lot of "one mores" that drove me on to keep gambling. We have two beautiful children together, a boy and a girl. Any parent knows the stress, both emotionally and financially, that children bring. I told myself the one mores were for my family, and I kept betting.

Each of those bets edged me closer to rock bottom. For me, there was not a single event that I can say was when I realized I had sunk as low as I could. Rock bottom, for me, was more like deciding that the job you've had for the last ten years is toxic and you need a change. I got to my rock bottom through a thousand little cuts. Each time I disappointed my family and friends was another tiny slice out of my soul.

Some of those cuts out of my spirit were bigger than others. When my daughter was little, I took $500 and parlayed it into a $45,000 win. I was still betting online with overseas sportsbooks back then. To get your winnings, the book had to wire the money into your bank account. That process always felt like it took forever. Being offshore, I was always scared they would never send my money. What would stop them from not honoring the bet? It's not like I could call the State Department up and complain an overseas gambling establishment didn't pay out.

Every day I would email the book and ask if my money had been sent. Two days prior they had told me the wire transfer had been initiated. A couple of times a day I would check on the money's status with my bank. Every time I'd call, the answer was the same, "No, Mr. Hatton, it hasn't come in. We'll let you know when it clears."

I didn't want to wait. Every minute I didn't have the payout in my hands was a minute lost I could be making more money. I'd just made an 8,900 percent profit, and who knows what else I could do with the money that was being wired to me. When the money finally came in on the fourth day, I was running errands with my wife and daughter. I told them I needed to make a stop at the bank, but I did not need to bother them with the details of what my business was.

"I won't be long," I told them and tried not to run across the parking lot.

A few minutes later I was in front of a teller with my ID and account number in hand. I could hear the clicks of the old school keyboard clack like the minute hand ticking on an old clock.

"Mr. Hatton, Mr. Hatton—did you bring anything to put the money in?"

It took me a second to realize that I could not just put that much money in my pockets. I must have given him the deer-in-the-headlights look because he took pity on me.

"I've got a paper bag here. Will that be sufficient?"

I nodded my head. I did not care if he put it in a burlap feed sack, whatever got me out of her quickest. Then the clerk started shucking out stacks of hundred dollar bills and lined them up as neat as soldiers across the counter. After I was satisfied at the count, I nodded, and the bills disappeared in the sack. The clerk was careful to fold over the paper at the top of the bag so no one could see the contents. I scurried across the parking lot to my car and popped the trunk. There was no reason to give my wife or daughter a chance to see what was in the bag. It would have only worried them.

That money could have been used for my daughter's college fund. I could have funded purchasing a rental house and gotten back into that game. I could have done any number of good things with the $45,000 sitting in my car's trunk, but I didn't. I lost every penny on the Seahawks and Patriots game. It was like I had lost more than an entire year's salary over a football game. The sad part was that it was not rock bottom. After that, I turned a $3,000 bet into $38,000. I lost that too. Over $80,000 I had thrown away when I should have walked away. I knew I had a problem, and I had to stop.

Recovery

I kept gambling even after those incredible losses. I wish one of those events had made me stop, but my soul slowly bleed out over those thousand cuts. I do not know exactly when or how, but the will to gamble started to fade. Every time I looked at my family, it gave me another reason to quit. Just like my rock bottom was due to a thousand cuts, my recovery was not me waking up one morning and not gambling. It was like a smoker decreasing the number of cigarettes he fired up in a day to ween himself off nicotine. Once I decided to quit, betting seemed more of a burden to me than a source of excitement.

Successful recovery is rarely a process that happens alone. If beating addiction was a solo effort, anyone who ever wanted to quit could do so. I went to a few Gamblers Anonymous meetings, but my greatest source of strength came from my church. I found that through prayer and discussing my compulsions with my pastor or fellow church members lightened my load. One of the suggestions that were given to me was to redirect the energy I put into gambling into something profitable. I decided to invest that energy back into my family.

Cupcakes and Hotdogs

Part of the way I wanted to invest in my family was to give them a good and early example of what being an entrepreneur is like. I thought when they were middle-school age, I could direct them to the standard jobs kids do—cutting grass, babysitting, raking leaves, and the like. My daughter, Sky, was well ahead of that curve. Since she was little every Sunday, she would spend the afternoons with her grandmother baking. By the time she was four, Sky was well on her way to being a good little pastry chef.

So, what does an enterprising young lady with a flair for baking want to do? Bake cupcakes and sell them. When she first presented the idea to me, I thought it was the "opening up a lemonade stand" phase every kid goes through. Then I thought this could be the introduction to business I had been looking for. I would help my four-year-old daughter open her own cupcake business. The first step for Sky's Cupcakes was to do market research. We all pitched in and experimented with different batters and frostings. Sky was the mastermind behind the flavor combinations. The quest was to produce the world's best cupcake. I don't know if we ever got close to a world-class cupcake, but the folks we initially shared them with sure did like them.

When we felt like we had a good mix of products, we started the sales and distribution phase. Unlike a lemonade stand where the business came to us, we decided to pitch our cupcakes directly. We visited cafes, senior centers, schools, and hospitals, giving out samples and hoping to take orders.

Wouldn't you know it, we started getting sales and media attention. Nashville's CBS affiliate, WTVF, even did a story about Sky's Cupcakes. Business got brisk enough that we had to hire a baker and use a commercial kitchen to fulfill orders.

Every step of the way, I explained to Sky what we were doing and why. I wanted to make sure she understood that the profits from this venture were being saved for her future. College, a down payment on a house, or whatever else she might need to make adulting a little easier. I wanted Sky to understand that dreams are all well and good, but ambition is nothing without hard work. Most important, I wanted my little girl to believe anything is possible. If you can own your own business at four, there's no limit to what you can do.

Working with Sky energized me. I thought about the emotional and financial drain gambling had been in my life compared to how good I felt working with my daughter. Every cupcake we sold made Sky smile and was one more reason for me never to gamble again. An addiction never fully goes away. The need to gamble starts to fade, and there are some days I don't even think about placing a bet. Other days, I get the itch to place a bet. The difference now is I can catch myself before that happens. I pray, call a friend, or do something to distract me until the compulsion passes.

Being in a headspace that was clear of gambling gave me time and energy to dream again. I started planning my reentry into real estate and one more foodservice venture. My brother-in-law had immigrated from Guyana a few years before and was interested in starting a business. We put our heads together and came up with a hook for a food truck. We'd call it the Hot Dog Mafia, and all of the menu items were named after famous gangsters. The Gotti had onions, kraut, spicy brown mustard, and was on a poppyseed bun. The El Chapo was a chili dog with nacho cheese and pico de gayo. To round out the menu, Sky dreamt up a signature cupcake, the Holy Canoli, that would only be available at Hot Dog Mafia. We had our soft opening at the Columbia Kroger and reporters from the *Daily Herald* were on hand to mark the occasion.

I like to think that success attracts success. Personally and professionally, I was on a roll. I was clean and living right. My family was at my side, and the world was running on greased grooves. There was nothing I wanted for other than the health and happiness of those around me. I had not consciously dropped the idea of real estate, but I wasn't actively pursuing it either. Then one day a gentleman struck up a conversation with me at Hot Dog Mafia. It turns out he was looking to develop a tract of land into a subdivision. The Lord places people in our lives at just the right time, and I would shortly be back in the real estate business.

Chapter Eight
Living in a Post-COVID World and the Future

The COVID-19 calamity of 2020 was as unexpected an event as having a sinkhole open in your front yard. There is not much that can be done about it other than react to the circumstance. I feared in the spring of 2020 that the housing market would go bust again like it did in 2007–8. The home improvement market was soaring as homeowners had nothing better to do than improve their living spaces. I thought this may translate into a dip in the housing market, and my present subdivision project may evaporate like tearing down the crack houses did. Other than a slight pause to wait out the astronomical rise in building material costs, the subdivision program is back on track.

Governmental Dependence and COVID

What does concern me about the government's reaction to COVID-19 is the fingerprint of dependence it will leave on our society. It is not that I don't believe we should help our fellow humans out in their time of need. Charity is one of the tenents of Christianity, and I believe those who need assistance should freely get it. What I do not believe in is gaming the system. The United States government has put several safeguards that protect those who cannot work during the pandemic.

One of these protections is suspended judicial and nonjudicial foreclosures in place in some states. That is a great piece of legislation intended to help those in dire financial straits. In the past few months, I've heard people say, "They can't kick me out of my apartment if I don't pay my rent, so I'm going to use my rent money to buy a bigger TV." That type of mentality is short-sighted and will only lead to heartache. You are eventually going to have to pay your rent or house note. When that day comes, you will be struggling to make up the difference.

Another thing to consider is that taking assistance when it is not needed takes away from someone who does need it. There are only so many dollars the government or any other organization has for charitable acts. Every dollar you take away from that pool of money reduces it for someone else. You might not agree with how the government taxes, or how the rich do not pay their fair share, but surfing on entitlements isn't how to address any of those grievances. Write your representatives and become part of the electoral process. Most importantly, go out and chase your dreams, so you do not have to worry about gaming the system.

One of the takeaways from my story should be that your fortunes can change on a dime—for good or bad. When you are in a low spot, don't give up. Look for ways to rise above your situation. That might look like getting a side hustle or learning a new skill by watching YouTube videos. Anything that moves you forward is not a waste of time. What is a waste of time is pointlessly scrolling through social media or engaging in any unprofitable behavior. I guarantee that you have got the intelligence and drive to achieve anything you desire. You just must convince yourself of that.

The other side of the coin is learning how to deal with success. You may think you've arrived when you hit certain goals, but do you have the internal maturity to deal with that success? Are you looking for another peak to climb? Are you planning for an exit strategy if everything around you crumbles tomorrow? Are you staying true to who you are and cherishing the values that got you to the top of this mountain? I did not. I thought that all of my hard work meant I deserved to take the shortcut of gambling. You see where that got me.

Legal Gambling in Tennessee

As I mentioned in the introduction, in 2020, the State of Tennessee legalized sports betting. You might think sports betting is like doing a March Madness board at work or putting a few dollars on a Super Bowl square—it's not. It does not matter if you don't develop a problem with gambling like I have. (A gambling addiction is like being an alcoholic. Being an addict is a continual state of being.) If you place a bet, you are fueling a machine you might not understand. Sport betting companies are in the business to make money—not to make you rich. As such, sports betting companies utilize strategies that either appear to minimize your risk or give perks for placing more bets. The more often you bet, the more likely you are to lose. Even if you can walk away from gambling, you have contributed to an organization that could ruin someone else's life.

Take the connection between sportsbook Action 24/7 and their sister company Advance Financial.[10] Advance Financial is a Tennessee company that offers high-interest-rate payday loans. The Tennessee Education Lottery's Sports Wagering Advisory Council, the governmental body in Tennessee that regulates gambling, allowed winnings from bets placed at Action 24/7 to be deposited in Advance Financial accounts to repay debt. Furthermore, Action 24/7 and Advance Financial operate at the same locations. This has caught the attention of Tennessee lawmakers. According to Tennessee State Representative Darren Jernigan:

> Currently, a person would be allowed to walk into an Advance Financial, get a loan for 279 percent interest, go to the next counter put that money into a sports wagering account to start betting. . . That

> is the literal definition of loan sharking, except the next day they don't go and break your legs, you get put into a cycle of debt that will end in bankruptcy.[11]

There is not much more to say about the ethics of the gaming industry than those business practices.

If you or a loved one has a gambling problem and don't know where to turn, Gambler's Anonymous is a good place to start. The organization was founded in California during the late 1950s and models itself on Alcoholics Anonymous' twelve-step program. To find a meeting or more about their support system, please visit www.gamblersanonymous.org.

Stocks and the Future

One of the avenues I had thought about going down earlier in my life was investing in stocks and being a financial advisor. About the time I was doing the *Mo' Money Monday* radio show, I caught the attention of Monty Sneed at Columbia's Caledonia Financial. I met with Monty a few times, and he tried to talk me into working for him. He was willing to buy the study guides and tutor me to pass my Series 7 Securities and Exchange Commission

(SEC) exam. This test is required to obtain a license to sell different financial products such as stocks and bonds. I turned Monty down because being a broker or financial advisor was not my passion then. Monty did, however, plant the seed of stock and bond investing in my mind. It was not until recently Monty's seed took root.

As this book is being written, I am working as a janitor at an industrial concern. The job isn't glamorous, but it is necessary for me to fuel my other ambitions. As chance, or divine providence, would have it, one of my coworkers had been investing in the stock market for years. Between him and Monty, I realized what I had been missing out on all these years. I could have been investing a portion of the cash I was saving for down payments in rental properties in stocks or bonds. That would grow those funds and allow me to make my down payment money faster.

I am relatively new to investing in the stock and bond markets. I will admit that the market was initially hard for me to wrap my mind around. Also, investing in something I can't see or touch is a hard sell for me too. With a house or piece of land, you can look at where your money is going. When you buy a municipal bond that's funding a construction project in Iowa or ownership in a company that makes trash bags, it's hard to see what your money is going toward. Once I started to understand how these financial instruments worked and the safeguards the SEC has in place, I dipped my toe in the water.

There is risk in the stock market, like any other investment. Even with this risk, I've been able to accelerate my plans. It will not be long before I'm working for myself full-time again and building a sustainable future for me and my family.

Closing

We are put here on this earth to build. God created us with a drive to improve on our surroundings. After all, isn't building anything just an improvement? A few bags of concrete, some wood, and nails by themselves are nothing. In a rain storm the concrete would harden in its bag, the wood would begin to rot, and the nails would be blown away with the wind. When you properly put all of the elements together, you can build a house that can withstand any storm. That's an improvement, wouldn't you say?

Psalms 118:22 tells us, "The stone the builders rejected has become the cornerstone." I interpret this verse to mean that at some points in our lives, we are unacceptable stones for the Great Builder. That does not mean that we will always have to be rough around the edges. We can always improve ourselves and become a foundation for better things. I like to think my, and your, life has been just that—a chance to improve and have the chance to do great things.

I would challenge you to take stock of what you want to build with your life. It's never too late and you're not so far gone that you cannot make positive changes in your life. If you take anything away from my story, it's that. Go, work hard, and build something because that is what we are called to do.

Appendix
Newspaper Clippings

The following pages contain articles that have been written about me over the years. I'd like to thank Columbia, Tennessee's *Daily Herald* and Jay Powell for his coverage and allowing me to reprint his articles.

Sky's Cupcakes Something Sweet for Everyone

By JAY POWELL

Posted Sep 3, 2018 at 10:36 AM

Updated Sep 3, 2018 at 8:08 PM

Sky Hatton, 4, stands with her father, James Hatton Jr. and brother, James Hatton III, 2, ready to fill an order of cupcakes for her business, Sky's Cupcakes. Her cupcakes were featured at the Maury County Fair and will be sold at local businesses around Columbia and Middle Tennessee. (Staff photo by Jay Powell)

Sky's Cupcakes can be ordered by calling (931) 255-3169. The company's slogan is: "Everybody needs a little sugar in their life."

It's never too early to learn about starting one's own business, and it helps when the product is something flavorful and delicious to satisfy the customer's sweet tooth.

Four-year-old Sky Hatton of Columbia is learning the ropes of entrepreneurship, and with great success, after recently founding her own baking company, Sky's Cupcakes, along with her parents James Jr. and Yolanda Hatton, and her grandmother, Sharmnitta Hatton.

After just a few months of creating fun and unique ideas, the business already has a growing customer base, and their cupcakes were a popular item sold at this year's Maury County Fair.

In addition to taking orders directly by calling (931) 255-3169, Sky's Cupcakes can be found at Bubba Gandy Seafood and Tallgrass Meat. Co., as well as Amber Falls Winery every other Saturday.

"We put a lot of time into making these cupcakes, creating the designs and making them homemade, never frozen or store bought," James Hatton Jr. said. "We don't use any cake mix, which is a little more expensive to make, but we want to make sure people are getting a good product. Even the icing is made from scratch."

Sky's love for baking began when she would watch cooking shows like Rachel Ray, Martha Stewart and "Cupcake Wars" on the Food Network, working alongside her grandmother in the kitchen and coming up with new ideas. Pretty soon the idea came about to start her own business and bring her tasty creations to the community.

“We’ve sold so many that we ran out of boxes last week,” Hatton said. “The sales are really high right now, between selling at the fair and taking calls. We had more calls than we expected, but we are prepared now to meet all orders.”

Sky’s cupcakes offers 10 unique flavors, such as grape Fanta, banana pudding, PB & J and Mississippi Mud. Cupcakes are sold for $20 per dozen, as well as “specialty flavors” like peach cobbler or Grandma Sharon’s Old Fashioned Caramel for $25 per dozen. There are also Sky’s Cupcakes T-shirts sold for $15 in all sizes and colors.

Sky said her favorite is the multi-colored rainbow flavor, and what she loves most about the business is getting to spend time cooking with her grandmother. Her other hobbies include taking ballet at Columbia Dance Academy and singing gospel songs at church, but her biggest passion is working in the kitchen and creating new ideas she hopes people can enjoy.

“I love baking cupcakes and getting to work with Grandma,” Sky Hatton said.

She also donates a portion of proceeds from the "pink velvet" flavor to charities for cancer research and prevention.

Her father said he is proud to watch his daughter's sense of entrepreneurship grow, instilling principles of working and supporting yourself at an early age, as well as how to manage money. Ten percent of sales is donated to the family's church, Christian Faith Church, and another 10 percent is placed in a trust fund, while the rest is either put back into the business or used for things like toys, because after all she still loves being a kid.

"We take 10 percent and give it to church for our tithes, because that's the most important part," Hatton said. "If she wants to go to college or be an entrepreneur, the money will be there when she turns 18. Most of this money is going to a college fund, or trust fund, that we have set up for her."

Having her own business at a young age is also a valuable skill he tries to instill in her for future success as she gets older, namely being able to take care of herself and to always have a willingness to work hard to succeed.

"I always tell people she's pretty like her mom, but gets her business ambition from me," Hatton said. "I want to support her in everything she does. And I talk to her and teach her that you want to create a good product and for your business to succeed, because you don't want to grow up and have the government take care of you, pay your bills and rent. I want her to be self-sufficient and understand that you don't have to depend on government programs to be successful in life."

Sky's Cupcakes recently launched a Facebook page, where customers can learn about flavors and keep track of local events where cupcakes will be sold. The Hattons have long-term plans to launch a full website later in the fall, where customers can make online orders through Paypal. They also hope to have a full-time food truck by March of next year.

There are also plans to bring her cupcakes to local schools, starting with Riverside Elementary where Sky attends pre-K, and Little Tikes Daycare, where she also attends.

"We'll go to places like Riverside or Highland Park Elementary, and we're going to hand out free cupcakes and business cards so people can actually taste the product, and if people have a birthday or just for any day they can order from us," Hatton said. "It's a really good cupcake, and we're very confident in what we're selling."

The main goal, other than developing a larger local customer base, is to move into a brick and mortar facility in downtown Columbia, and eventually open in multiple locations in Spring Hill and other Middle Tennessee areas.

"We want to have a Sky's Cupcakes in every county in Middle Tennessee over the next 5-10 years. That's our plan," Hatton said. "Our slogan is 'Everybody needs some sugar in their life,' and we're just trying to provide that part."

Hot Dog Mafia Dangerously Delicious

By JAY POWELL
Posted Apr 16, 2019 at 10:57 AM
Updated Apr 16, 2019 at 4:57 PM

From left, Jevon London and James Hatton serve up fresh hot dogs at their Hot Dog Mafia stand in the Kroger parking lot off James M. Campbell Boulevard. The hot dog stand serves up gourmet franks based on historic crime bosses and their country of origin. (Staff photo by Jay Powell)

James Hatton puts the final touches on the El Chapo dog, which features chili, nacho cheese, pico de gayo, sour cream and sliced jalapenos.

Hot Dog Mafia is located in the Kroger parking lot off James M. Campbell Boulevard. (Staff photos by Jay Powell)

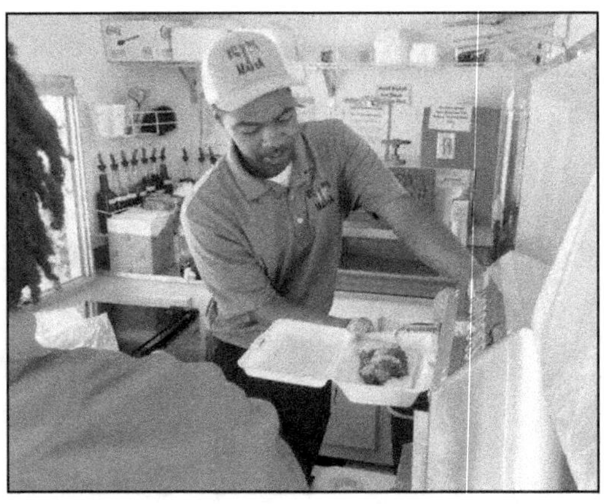

There's a new food truck in Columbia, one that'll make you an offer you can't refuse.

Hot Dog Mafia, a new hot dog stand began serving its gourmet links earlier this week, hosting a soft opening at the Kroger off James Campbell Boulevard. The business is a partnership between James Hatton, who's daughter Sky Hatton runs her own popular cupcake business, and his brother-in-law, Jevon London.

The business specializes in its namesake, but with a certain old world twist. Each hot dog featured on the menu is modeled after a particular crime boss from the past, with toppings based on their region of origin.

For instance, "The Gotti" features spicy brown mustard, sauerkraut and sauteed onions on a steamed poppyseed bun. The "El Chapo," which so far has been the stand's best seller, includes chili, nacho cheese, pico de gayo, sour cream and sliced jalapeños. All of the buns are steamed and baked fresh every morning by Windmill Bakery.

"We've got hot dogs from all over the entire world, from Chicago to Mexico all the way to the country of Colombia," Hatton said. "Our toppings range from baked beans to pineapple. Everything is totally different."

The idea to open a hot dog stand wasn't just to provide Columbia residents with a tasty new eatery destination, but a chance for one of its owners to have his own business. London is a native of Guyana in South America, having moved to the United States in 2016. He said he is grateful for the opportunity, especially after the long and arduous process it took to become a legitimate citizen.

"I work for Walmart, and this is a breath of fresh air to do something I like. The opportunity here in America is good, that's why I like it, because where I come from there isn't much opportunity," London said. "The economy is so low, and tourism wise, since it's near the Caribbean, does well."

He said it was through his mother that he was able to get a green card, secure citizenship and begin a new life for himself.

"My mom's been here for a while, and thanks to her she applied for me," London said. "I'm really thankful."

Hot Dog Mafia also has a few treats in store for anyone who's tried one of Sky's Cupcakes. The stand sells its own exclusive, "Holy Canoli" cupcake, which features cream cheese, milk chocolate and bits of canoli. There are also 19 flavors of sno-cones to bite into on a hot day.

Hot Dog Mafia will partner with Riverside Elementary, hosting a special fundraising event next Monday, April 22 from 5-7 p.m. Ten percent of all proceeds will be donated back to the school, while the homeroom that raises the most money in sales will win a sno-cone coupon.

"We're going to give back 10 percent to the schools from that," Hatton said.

Although this week is a soft opening for the business, Hatton said Hot Dog Mafia will be in the James Campbell Kroger parking lot from 10 a.m. to 7 p.m., starting May 1.

There are also plans to make appearances at upcoming community events, festivals and possibly expanding to other areas.

“We want to be at festivals, maybe open another location down the road,” London said.

Hatton Hills Project to Create Luxurious, Affordable Homes

By JAY POWELL
Posted Jul 24, 2019 at 11:26 AM
Updated Jul 24, 2019 at 6:09 PM

A rendering of the proposed Hatton Hills project, spearheaded by James Hatton of Columbia in an effort to create housing on West 4th Street.

There's a certain pride that comes from giving back to one's community, especially when it means building homes that are not only luxurious, but affordable.

James Hatton, a Columbia native who readers might remember as the father of Sky Hatton, the five-year-old entrepreneur of Sky's Cupcakes. He is also co-founder of the Hot Dog Mafia food truck. Hatton is now spearheading another ambitious project for Columbia by building a brand new subdivision just south of the downtown square.

The proposed Hatton Hills will consist of between 15-19 homes built on 5.5 acres along West 4th Street. Hatton said he hopes to create an affordable place to live that will continue to grow, while breathing new life into an area ripe for development. He also said he believes now is the perfect time to invest in real estate given the current state of growth the city is experiencing.

"The reason I'm doing this is so I can have my own business, and for a profit, but more importantly I want to provide luxurious houses at affordable prices for the neighborhood and also for the city of Columbia," Hatton said. "Columbia is doing really great right now, and I want to do my part in helping Columbia be beautiful again."

Hatton's passion for real estate goes back to when he was 18 years old, working two jobs at McDonald's and putting in 80-hour work weeks. Through saving money, hard work and dedication, he was able to buy his first house.

"It was from hard work, working at two fast food chains 80 hours a week, saving money, putting it back so I can buy my first house when I was 18 years old. Now, I want to provide people who are married, or to help a family by giving them a beautiful home at a price they can afford. I'm not about trying to get rich off of someone else, but just provide a good product.

And when it comes to providing good real estate, it always comes back to location, location, location.

"This is in a very good location on West 4th Street. It's close to the Riverwalk and is walking distance to 6th Street going into downtown Columbia," Hatton said. "You're also close to McDowell Elementary and Columbia Academy, so you're getting the best of both worlds."

He came into ownership of the West 4th Street property through what he calls "a gift from God." The property was originally planned to develop into a megachurch by Word of Life Ministry. The original owner, Pastor Steve Gray, passed away in 2012, leaving the project unfinished. Pastor Gray's wife, Mamie, who also preaches at the Columbia church, sold Hatton the property after he shared his vision for what he hoped to do with it.

"It was a real blessing, and I pray to God every night to give me the opportunity to do what I love to do," Hatton said. "It so happened this was for sale, and God did the rest. It touched her heart, and she said if Pastor Gray was still here he would want me to have this patch of land to do what I plan on doing."

Hatton Hills is set to break ground in late-September/early-October, and each house will include four bedrooms, two-and-a-half baths, a one-and-a-half car garage and built using brick foundations and a hardy board exterior. Each home will list in the mid-$200K range and sold through United Country Real Estate, and will go up for sale in about six weeks. The estimated build time, he said, will be about 90 days, wrapping up construction around the holiday season.

Those interested in possibly purchasing a Hatton Hills home can contact Amy Carlton at United Country at (931) 374-8485. Hatton said he expects the homes to sell fast, and the sooner a potential buyer inquires interest the better, mainly because there will be time to request custom design work.

Hatton also has a similar project, Hatton Village, planned over 14 acres in Lawrenceburg near Lawrenceburg High School. He is also venturing into the podcast world later this fall, where he hopes to share with listeners his advice on finance, real estate and how he was able to pursue his passions, one day hopefully turning them into a full time job.

"When you start your own business and do things you are passionate about, it's not really a job," Hatton said. "It just becomes a hobby you get paid for, which I think is what everyone wants."

'James Hatton Jr. Show' to Tackle Real Estate and Wealth Building on Wkom

JAY POWELL | THE DAILY HERALD |
11:01 pm CDT July 3, 2020

James Hatton Jr. will debut his new show, "The James Hatton Jr. Show" at 4:30 p.m. Monday on WKOM 101.7 FM. The show will delve into topics regarding personal finance, real estate and business. He is also in the process of publishing a new book, "From Flipping Burgers to Flipping Billions," which chronicles the lessons he has learned over the years as an entrepreneur and self-made business owner.

Everyone loves a good success story, but it's even more inspiring when it's someone who had it all, lost it all and found their way back to redemption stronger than ever.

That's the story of James Hatton Jr.'s journey in achieving his own successes, while also living by an example for his children and others he can teach. Listeners to WKOM 101.7 FM will soon hear his story, as well as his take on handling personal finances, investing, real estate and how to avoid the pitfalls of money. "The James Hatton Jr. Show" is scheduled to debut on the station for a weekly half-hour spot starting at 4:30 p.m. Monday.

Daily Herald readers might remember Hatton, or more particularly his daughter, Sky, who at 5 years old created her own bakery business, Sky's Cupcakes, which he said is "prepping for a huge announcement" this fall.

One thing I've always admired about Hatton is his openness in sharing the lessons he's learned over the years, starting as a young entrepreneur flipping burgers at multiple jobs, amassing his own empire in real estate and the guidance he received from mentors along the way. He also talks openly about the mistakes he made, getting tied up in the world of gambling, which ultimately led to him losing everything.

It's hard to wrap your brain around a statement like, "I lost $65,000 betting on a sports game," but that's part of his story, and the real horrors that are out there when someone carrying such a weighty responsibility gets greedy. However, part of the "success story" is how one learns from their mistakes, and instead uses them as a tool to become a better person who, hopefully, educates others in how to avoid them.

That's what this new radio show is about, and but I think that's only the tip of the iceberg in what a local finance/real estate talk show can offer the community. It's another step in how our local radio station continues to develop the kind of hyperlocal content that's not only entertaining, but the type of information people can benefit from hearing.

"The format is all about business and money, and I'm going to have guests ranging from pastors to realtors, bankers, financial advisors," Hatton said. "When you think about it, a lot of Americans will put a lot of money into things like their health, but not a lot really think about putting it into financials. "

Station owner Delk Kennedy said he continues to be amazed at the progress WKRM/WKOM has made since taking ownership and reformatting its programming earlier this year. His goal from the start has been to produce as much locally-produced content for the station's airwaves as possible. The success has come in the form of providing a good balance of news, talk radio, music and sports.

Having a show which focuses on real estate growth in Maury County seemed like a natural fit, and one that listeners can tune into each week and learn something beneficial, as well as highly relevant, to the current state of the county.

"From the beginning, we said we want to be hyper-local, that we are a community radio station, and certainly one of the aspects of that is what's happening in our local real estate market," Kennedy said. "Columbia and Maury County are growing, and the way we live is changing. I expect James will speak to that, as well as the fundamentals on things like how to shop for a house, how to price it, that kind of thing. And he also talks about wealth building through real estate."

The community remains one of the fastest developing areas in the state, which certainly deserves its spotlight, especially when its done in a way that can be easily digested. This includes real estate, developing small businesses, manufacturing and arts culture. With so much activity happening in the community, along with the way businesses have adapted during the COVID-19 crisis, one thing is certain. The "The James Hatton Jr. Show" will have no shortage of guests or discussion topics.

The main thing Hatton hopes to connect with listeners on is how handling finances and making money isn't as hard as people might think it is. It just takes the right tools, guidance and understanding of the various markets, but that a lot of it comes down to the fact people "just don't know how to do it."

"A lot of people, especially around here, spend a lot of their money on scratch-off [lottery tickets] trying to get rich, but there are so many other ways you can get rich that doesn't involve gambling, like stocks, indexes, commodities," Hatton said. "But you have to understand how to do these things, how to apply them and make them happen. That's the purpose of this show, to get the information out where people can understand X, Y and Z and get the money they are looking for without doing anything unethical."

Hatton is also in the process of publishing his story in a book, "From Flipping Burgers to Flipping Billions," which he hopes to release by the end of the year. Other projects he has in the works include a podcast and launching a website. No matter the medium, each will involve Hatton sharing his story, his advice and the skills he learned about how to make money, and earning it the honorable way.

"It tells of all the peaks and valleys of what I went through, going from one to the other and eventually succeeding. Because I lost a lot of money, was greedy and started doing things that were completely unethical with high-stakes gambling," Hatton said. "I'd like to take it and speak at local fast food restaurants, because that's where I got my start. I want them to know that 'you too can make something of yourself, even if it starts here flipping burgers.'"

Endnotes

[1] City Data, 2020.

[2] Lee, 2019.

[3] This example does not take into account interest charged on a loan. Typical loans are set up so that your initial payments go towards reducing your interest debit and extraordinarily little of your loan payment goes towards the loan's principle or building equity in a home. If you're taking out a home loan, you can ask your banker for an amortization table that will tell you how much interest and principle you're paying for the life of the loan.

[4] United States Department of Labor, 2021.

[5] Kim P., 2019. These represent the national gas prices per gallon for those years.

[6] Dimburg, 2019.

[7] United States Social Security Administration, 2019.

[8] Trump, 2021.

[9] Amedo, 2020. Fannie Mae and Freddie Mac are the informal names for the Federal National Mortgage Association (FNMA) and Federal Home Loan Mortgage Corporation (FMLMC) respectively.

[10] Elliot, 2020. Elliot's article in the *Nashville Post* states: "Tennessee Action 24/7 is led by executives from Nashville-based payday loan provider Advance Financial. According to Securities and Exchange Commission filings, Advance Financial CFO Patrick Conroy and Andrew Jacks, a former senior director at Advance, are executive officers for Tennessee Action 24/7. Advance Financial President and CEO Tina Hodges is also listed as a director of Tennessee Action 24/7."

[11] Harris, 2021.

Bibliography

Amadeo, Kimberly. "2008 Financial Crisis Causes, Costs, and Could It Happen Again?" The Balance, October 30, 2020. https://tinyurl.com/586nzpaw.

Amadeo, Kimberly. "How Derivatives Could Trigger Another Financial Crisis." The Balance. Accessed April 5, 2021. https://www.thebalance.com/role-of-derivatives-in-creating-mortgage-crisis-3970477.

Amadeo, Kimberly. "What Happened During the Auto Industry Bailout?" The Balance, June 29, 2020. https://www.thebalance.com/auto-industry-bailout-gm-ford-chrysler-3305670.

Back Yard Burgers. "Back Yard Burgers in USA." Back Yard Burgers. Quick Serve Restaurants in the United States. Accessed February 24, 2021. https://www.backyard-burgers.com/our-story/.

BetMGM. "Jamie Foxx To Star In BetMGM's New Brand Campaign." BetMGM, September 24, 2020. https://sports.betmgm.com/en/blog/jamie-foxx-betmgm-campaign/.

City Data. "Crime Rate in Columbia, Tennessee (TN): Murders, Rapes, Robberies, Assaults, Burglaries, Thefts, Auto Thefts, Arson, Law Enforcement Employees, Police Officers, Crime Map." Crime in Columbia, Tennessee (TN): murders, rapes, robberies, assaults, burglaries, thefts, auto thefts, arson, law enforcement employees, police officers, crime map. Accessed January 27, 2021. https://tinyurl.com/v5bvhz59.

City of Columbia. "Home." Home - City of Columbia. Accessed January 27, 2021. https://www.columbiatn.com/.

DePietro, Andrew. "Banks That Are Suspending Foreclosures During Coronavirus Crisis." Forbes. Forbes Magazine, December 15, 2020. https://www.forbes.com/sites/andrewdepietro/2020/03/31/banks-suspending-foreclosures-covid-19/?sh=52392ed22 20c.

Dimberg, Kelsey Rae. "This Is What Groceries Cost the Year You Were Born." Taste of Home. Taste of Home, June 26, 2019. https://www.tasteofhome.com/collection/this-is-what-groceries-cost-the-year-you-were-born/.

Elliot, Stephen. "Advance Financial Officials behind Sports Betting Outfit," August 25, 2020. https://www.nashvillepost.com/sports/article/21143002/advance-financial-officials-behind-sports-betting-outfit.

Elliot, Stephen. "Sportsbook with Advance Financial Connections Suspended." *Nashville Post*, March 19, 2021. https://www.nashvillepost.com/sports/sports-business/

article/21146653/sportsbook-with-advance-financial-connections-suspended.

Federal Housing Finance Agency. "Get Started Here:" About Fannie Mae & Freddie Mac | Federal Housing Finance Agency. Accessed April 2, 2021. https://www.fhfa.gov/SupervisionRegulation/FannieMaeandFreddieMac/Pages/About-Fannie-Mae---Freddie-Mac.aspx.

Fleeman, Johnny. "History of Johnny Fleeman." Johnny Fleeman's Gourmet Foods - Home. Accessed April 6, 2021. http://www.johnnyfleeman.com/v/vspfiles/jfg/history.html.

Frodin, Jon. "Burn the Ships: Hernán Cortés and the Order That Changed the New World." OnePeterFive, August 27, 2018. https://tinyurl.com/y9yfmna5.

Harris, Gerald. "TN Lawmakers File Bill to Stop You from Getting a Payday Loan and Waging a Bet at the Same Place." WKRN News 2. WKRN News 2, February 26, 2021. https://www.wkrn.com/news/tennessee-news/tn-lawmakers-file-bill-to-stop-you-from-getting-a-payday-loan-and-waging-a-bet-at-the-same-place/.

P., Kim. "Gas Price History." CreditDonkey. CreditDonkey, November 21, 2019. https://www.creditdonkey.com/gas-price-history.html.

Rennick, Lee. "The Maryland Farms Office Park Controversy," April 26, 2019. https://williamsonsource.com/history-maryland-farms-brentwood-tennessee/.

Skovira, Kristen. "4-Year-Old Launches Sky's Cupcakes." WTVF, November 12, 2018. https://www.newschannel5.com/news/4-year-old-cake-boss-launches-sky-cupcakes-with-the-help-of-her-family.

Tennessean. "James Morris Daughty Obituary." September 1, 2011. https://obits.tennessean.com/obituaries/tennessean/obituary.aspx?pid=153390535.

The Street Staff. Tax Deductions for Rental Property Depreciation. MSN. Accessed April 3, 2021. https://tinyurl.com/35ad9ahb.

Trump, Donald. *TRUMP: The Art of the Deal*. New York, NY: Random House Business, 2020.

United States Department of Labor. "History of Federal Minimum Wage Rates Under the Fair Labor Standards Act, 1938 - 2009." U.S. Department of Labor Seal. Accessed March 9, 2021. https://www.dol.gov/agencies/whd/minimum-wage/history/chart.

United States Social Security Administration. "Social Security." Average Wage Index (AWI). Accessed March 9, 2021. https://www.ssa.gov/oact/cola/awidevelop.html.

www.ingramcontent.com/pod-product-compliance
Lightning Source LLC
LaVergne TN
LVHW010059110826
845155LV00028B/405

* 9 7 8 1 9 4 4 0 6 6 4 3 7 *